DIAMOND BARATTA DESIGN

WILLIAM DIAMOND AND ANTHONY BARATTA
WRITTEN BY DAN SHAW

BULFINCH PRESS
NEW YORK · BOSTON

CONTENTS

BARBER SHOP

INTRODUCTION

WHEN WE SAT DOWN AFTER WORKING TOGETHER FOR TWENTY-five years to select the photographs for this book, we did not know what we would discover about ourselves. We knew that we were versatile designers whose enthusiasms ranged from modernism to eighteenth-century France, from chinoiserie to American folk art, and we wondered if there was a common thread that defined our career. What became apparent to us was that the most important feature in each of the twenty-four projects in this book is the way our clients' personalities and passions are reflected in their homes. Decorating for us is a collaborative process. We think of our clients as partners and muses and see ourselves as interpreters of their dreams by listening very carefully to them. We like to do what we have not done before, weaving together a dynamic and divergent aesthetic vocabulary to conceive one-of-a kind interiors.

To design unique residences we rely heavily on custom work. We have developed an extensive network of craftspeople and artisans who use Old World techniques to make furnishings for today: weavers, textile printers, muralists, braiders, needlepointers, upholsterers, quilters, embroiderers, and cabinetmakers. With the expertise of these men and women we can create the unexpected, such as the idiosyncratic "theme" houses where flowers, bumblebees, sailing ships, or Labradors are the leitmotif. We love color, and our unique use of it brings our clients great joy. Because we do so much couture work, we can specify the exact shades we want and apply them in new ways and daring combinations throughout the house. Our control over color lets us layer pattern on pattern in a harmonious way.

The sense that everything is balanced and fine-tuned in our rooms is also due to the fact that we almost always do the architecture as well. In most of our projects, we simultaneously formulate the floor plan and the elevations while we conceptualize the decorating. Whether the architecture is modernist or classical, it is integral to the design scheme, the backbone of every project. We love nothing more than reinterpreting the past by transforming something pedestrian like Early American braided rugs into astonishing modern floor coverings in colors and patterns that are as compelling as the best abstract paintings. We've given new meaning and relevance to houndstooth, argyle, tweed, harlequin, and tartan by having them woven in bold colors and proportions and therefore transforming these familiar fabrics into Pop Art.

Our work has been celebrated as well as criticized over the past quarter century that we have worked together, but we have always followed our vision. What we offer our clients is timeless: comfortable houses infused with positive energy. Our clients are like family, and we know we are fortunate that they support us professionally as well as personally; they are patrons in the truest sense. We hope this book finds a place in the homes of everyone who cares about architecture and design, and that it inspires people who love beautiful homes to dream out loud. We are lucky enough to do that every day, and we highly recommend it.

—William Diamond and Anthony Baratta
New York City

YOUNG
MODERNS

WHEN A YOUNG ART-COLLECTING COUPLE APPROACHED us, they explained that they wanted their six-story Manhattan townhouse to be classically elegant but not serious or stuffy. We considered it an unusual challenge: could we devise cunning, colorful rooms that did not overwhelm the owners' modern paintings (such as the Joan Mitchell, opposite, that we hung in the foyer)? We were asked to do the architecture as well as the decorating, which gave us the opportunity to open up the living room and install exquisite moldings, mantels, and archways that would form a nuanced, timeless backdrop for art and furniture with strong character.

Naturally the owners had rules and restrictions — they wanted the color blue to predominate but were not fond of bold-patterned fabrics — which meant we would have to be quietly inventive to make the rooms engaging and dynamic. We decided that graphic rugs would have a starring role; inspired by twentieth-century paintings by Piet Mondrian, Josef Albers, and Frank Stella, the floor coverings are bold, one-of-a-kind works of art themselves — as well as wondrous conversation pieces that provide a sly, sophisticated leitmotif.

Our favorite room may be the master bath and dressing room. With oceanic, reverse-painted glass walls; a custom, nickel-plated dressing table and vanity; and pure white marble floors and counters, it manages to be both understated and over the top, a perfect balance that is the essence of style.

A Paul Mathieu bench with a gray suede cushion sits beneath a painting by Joan Mitchell. Paintings by Frank Stella inspired the design of the carpet.

The living room is a marriage of modern and traditional. Our fabric choices prevented the cool blue palette from making the room feel chilly. Based on a 1950s Italian design, the seating group on the right is covered in a blue-gray suede that was quilted to give it extra depth and character. The love seat is upholstered in a richly textured, handwoven geometric pattern; woven blowups of one square of the fabric create the throw pillows. Over the fireplace hangs an R. B. Kitaj painting. The Roman shades are checkerboard-pattern lace sheers.

FOLLOWING PAGE LEFT: We designed the living-room rug after the early paintings of Piet Mondrian and tried to mimic the look of the artist's brushstrokes in the weave.

FOLLOWING PAGE RIGHT: Eleven-foot-tall bookcases are framed by classical pilasters, a stoic counterpoint to the modern furniture. The throw pillows are a silk patchwork riff on 1960s geometric paintings. We designed the black lacquer coffee table.

OPPOSITE: A 1960s Fontana Arte mirror hangs over a nineteenth-century marble-topped walnut chest.

THIS PAGE: A variety of materials keeps the formal dining room from feeling austere. Luscious gray velvet covers the walls, and the diamond quilted draperies are soigné gray silk satin. The chairs have rich cobalt blue velvet seats, a nod to the magnificent antique blue-glass chandelier over the round custom-design tiger-maple table. Another early work by the painter Piet Mondrian inspired the rug.

OPPOSITE: The geometric-pattern rug and the needle-point throw pillow were designed for the library.
THIS PAGE: We tweaked tradition by designing Biedermeier-inspired bookcases and a crazy-cove ceiling in tiger maple (instead of the predictable oak or mahogany); upholstering the sofa in a custom-colored glen plaid that no one in Scotland would recognize; designing a free-form terrazzo coffee table with sculptural steel legs; and hanging a giant photograph of the Rolling Stones on the felt wall behind the sofa.

The white-on-white kitchen is enlivened by a plaid floor in white, gray, and black marble checkerboard squares and modernist chairs with blue leather seats.
OPPOSITE: The butler's pantry has mahogany cabinets with patterned glass doors and two-inch-thick white Carrara marble counters.

For bathroom walls we like to use reverse-painted glass because it has a color and depth that mimic the sea. The tub is surrounded by pure white marble, and the round window echoes the round domed skylight above.
OPPOSITE: We think there's nothing more glamorous than the nickel-plated dressing table, mirrors, and vanities with marble countertops that we designed especially for this room.

WHEN IT COMES TO OUR OWN HOMES, WE ALWAYS collaborate with each other, and our work on Tony's new loft reflects an evolution and synthesis of his wide-ranging tastes. Whereas his previous homes featured strong color statements — red and green; orange, chartreuse, and magenta; black and white with turquoise and pink — this place was a chance for us to explore the richness and complexities of masculine neutrals like camel hair, gray flannel, and saddle leather. It was also an opportunity to work with our second Lee Jofa fabric collection, which features reinterpretations of menswear standards like houndstooth and tweed in new colorations and proportions. By creating a relatively sober backdrop for Tony's diverse collections — Art Deco, mid-century, and Victorian furniture, along with nineteenth-century plaster casts and photographs — we managed to create a sense of discipline and order while honoring his individualistic, eclectic spirit.

OPPOSITE: We found the floor lamp in Canada and had it painted black and white; we reproduced it when we decorated the Eden Roc Hotel in Miami Beach. THIS PAGE: The custom cabinet is a handmade replica of a nineteenth-century cast-iron building indigenous to Tony's neighborhood; it conceals a flat-screen TV. The chair is upholstered in a giraffe-print pony skin.

Exaggerated shapes from a variety of periods live together harmoniously in the living room. The Harlequin lamp and magnificently proportioned eight-foot-long Victorian sofa, which was reupholstered in saddle leather, were used in previous apartments. The height of the back of the 1960s teak chair (to the left of the sofa) was raised to give it the right scale; the fiberglass-and-metal chair (to the right of the sofa) was designed by Estelle & Irwin Laverne in the 1960s and evokes Eero Saarinen's legendary TWA terminal at JFK Airport. Beneath everything is a braided rug that was fashioned from menswear fabrics such as tweed, herringbone, houndstooth, camel hair, and gray flannel. Custom-embroidered trim on the linen curtains recalls the designs of Josef Hoffmann.

OPPOSITE: "Bat Chair" is the name we gave our amplified version of a Deco classic; it's covered in a dimensional linen houndstooth of black, linen, and camel. The plaster cast is part of Tony's extensive collection of nineteenth-century nudes, which were used by art schools and museums when they could not get real marble sculptures for study or exhibition.

THIS PAGE: Tony also collects photographs of plaster casts, which are displayed in a custom folding screen. We are crazy for the dining chairs that were inspired by ones we saw in London, although ours have dramatically higher backs.

OPPOSITE: One side of the mirror, which we purchased in New Orleans, is a wood marquetry portrait of a young Arnold Schwarzenegger. Guglielmo Ulrich's vintage chair has its original zebra covering. The black, white, and camel carpet was a custom design for the loft, which is now part of our collection for Stark.

THIS PAGE: Two rococo Belter-style settees that had been in Tony's Miami apartment were torn apart to create a footboard and headboard for the king-size bed. The saddle-leather upholstery and black-and-white welting were also used on the living-room sofa and dining-room chairs. The duvet at the foot of the bed is made from our Elijah menswear patchwork fabric for Lee Jofa.

LIKE MANY WOMEN WHO WORK IN THE FASHION industry, this cosmopolitan client is enamored of Paris, and she wanted her New York penthouse to evoke her favorite city. Although the apartment is in an Art Deco building that dates back to the 1930s (a wonderful time for French interiors), we had to gut it first because it hadn't been updated in more than half a century. When we put it back together, we created a chic shell — pale pink walls, shiny black floors, low bookcases — that would be a stylish Deco backdrop for curvaceous furniture and her small, but growing, contemporary-art collection. We added a new mantel inspired by the plaster ones that were Dorothy Draper's signature in the 1930s.

Ironically, our client's mother is a decorator whom we revere and who's famous for her profuse layering of floral and plaid fabrics. In the spirit of rebellion, her daughter wanted something very different from what she had grown up with. She craved a simple, controlled environment without frills or excess. We respected her wishes, but we couldn't help ourselves in the bedroom: we encouraged her to buy the large flower painting that hangs over the bed, which we then dressed in ultrafeminine, floral D. Porthault linens from France. The result is dreamy, enchanting, and *trés jolie.*

Chartreuse, blue-green, and black were combined in different proportions for the terrazzo coffee table, the three differently woven round "polka-dot" braided rugs, and the Chanel-like tweed fabric on the armchair. The dining chairs are 1960s Italian with blue-green leather seats embellished with nail heads.

Visitors are often shocked by this Manhattan penthouse, for the contrast with the grayness of the cityscape below is both profound and refreshing. A few well-chosen vintage pieces — Art Deco emerald-and-clear-glass sconces, a Venetian mirror, outdoor wire furniture that we found in London — give the pale pink living room a Continental air. The cushions are ribbed turquoise ottoman cloth embroidered with a Matisse diamond grid. The curved back of the sofa follows the line of the round rug beneath it. We found the old bird cage at a flea market and turned it into a standing lamp. Video artist Nam June Paik made the drawing on the wall. The picture reflected in the mirror is an Andy Warhol print of Sarah Bernhardt.

Our inspiration for the chaise was Napoleon III; the custom-woven fabric resembles a tweed Chanel suit, a subtle expression of our client's love of French fashion. The harlequin-patterned carpet is one of our linchpins and is undeniably modern and feminine in this coloration.

OPPOSITE: One of our favorite art dealers was the late Holly Solomon, who championed avant-garde artists. We found White Zinnia by Jean Lowe at her legendary Soho gallery; the elaborate frame is part of the work. The Louis XV headboard is upholstered in gauffrage velvet and trimmed with pewter nail heads. The romantic French sheets are from D. Porthault.

SOMETIMES ONE SERENDIPITOUS PURCHASE SETS the course for an entire project. In the case of this Tribeca loft, it was a set of vintage, pull-down topographic school maps that we found at one of our favorite haunts, the tri-annual Brimfield Antiques Show in Massachusetts. We were attracted to the maps by their graphic quality and took them off the rollers and framed them individually. We also admired their strong, pure hues — bright green, turquoise, and orange — and opted to use them throughout the loft since our newlywed clients had told us they wanted their home to be colorful and playful. But first we had to tweak the architecture by adding nineteenth-century details such as pressed-tin ceilings and tin crown moldings so the loft would regain its historic, local character.

Once we had organized the space — carving out a bedroom, a library, and a kitchen with massive French doors — we painted all the floors with high-gloss turquoise deck paint. Then, letting the maps guide us, we looked for furniture and accessories with a schoolhouse aesthetic, adding in some modernist classics by Arne Jacobsen and Vladimir Kagan, along with a few good, solid antiques. Energized by mixing metaphors, we had a giant houndstooth fabric woven for the living-room sofa which established a new class of overblown traditional fabrics.

A pair of biology-lab stools stands in front of the pacesetting school maps framed like fine art. In the foreground one of Vladimir Kagan's highly collectible indoor-outdoor chairs from his 1958 Capricorn collection sits on a rug that's an homage to Pop Art. Vintage globes are displayed on an antique sculptor's table to which we added a scalloped leather apron. We had Robert Indiana's famous LOVE logo needlepointed for a pillow in the school-map colors.

The base of the dining table is made from a nineteenth-century architect's table; we added a new marble top and surrounded it with iconic Arne Jacobsen chairs. Michael Howard's painting of the Statue of Liberty depicts the owners' downtown neighborhood.
OPPOSITE: We sliced a crotch-mahogany Empire settee in half as if it were a Kaiser roll to create the bed, which we trimmed in ribbed velvet and French natural nail heads. The nightstand is an antique American sewing table. Innovative Denyse Schmidt made the modern, couture patchwork quilt.

In the library a high-spirited custom carpet (also opposite) tells the story of the couple's life together so far. References allude to his love of basketball and vintage pickup trucks; the diamond represents their wedding; the daisy symbolizes that they're children of the 1960s. OPPOSITE: New tin moldings are set off by walls covered in teal billiard cloth. The Victorian cabinet was found in New Orleans, which has always been a good source for oversize furniture. Whimsical Gothic felt appliqués decorate the Deco club chairs.

EIGHTEEN YEARS AFTER WE FIRST HELPED CLIENTS decorate their full-floor Fifth Avenue apartment in a traditional style with eighteenth-century American antiques, they called to tell us that they'd just bought the apartment below and needed our help to combine the two spaces. "I want to go modern," said the wife, "I want it to feel like a loft." Needless to say she is not your typical uptown matron; indeed, she's a bit of a maverick who follows her own rules.

Passionate about domestic life and fully involved in the lives of her children and three dogs, she wanted the apartment to be functional, not fussy; gracious, but not grandiose. She loves to cook, so the design of the kitchen was very important. To effortlessly accommodate a crowd, we created a massive living room that's forty feet long by thirty feet wide and as comfortable as a den. It is ringed by bookshelves filled with thousands of books, including humble paperbacks, for these clients don't decorate to impress others.

Since the apartment has only east and west exposures and isn't always flooded with natural light, she insisted that the walls be painted the purest white to keep everything bright, clean, and contemporary. The soft modernism we created was tailored for their lifestyle. As always with these clients, our collaboration brought unexpected and stunning results.

A twentieth-century chrome
chair that collapses into a cot is a
prime example of metamorphic
furniture; we added saddle leather
to the arms and cushions in a
handwoven tattersall fabric. The
end table is Warren Platner's wire
classic by Knoll. Our client had
the clever notion of asking
us to reinvent the simple Indian
dhurrie in two shades of blue-
green, gray, white, and camel.

OPPOSITE: A Shaker-inspired staircase poetically links the old apartment with the new one. The banister is mahogany, and the floors are bleached oak.

THIS PAGE: Antique metal shelving units from a French post office dominate the foyer and are used to hold everyday items like mail, homework, dog leashes, and mittens. The rug is our blown-up version of a 1950s textile by Lucienne Day, one of Britain's most influential modernist designers.

Antique English pine paneling on the two-story wall that bridges the floors adds an element of old-world warmth but has a relaxed, modern attitude because of the scale of the giant horizontal boards. The golfing portrait by eminent Scottish painter Sir John Watson Gordon reflects the husband's favorite sport. The eighteenth-century Connecticut secretary was purchased for the first incarnation of the apartment from the legendary antiques dealer Fred J. Johnston, whose house and showroom in Kingston, New York, are now a public museum.

FOLLOWING PAGE: Low-to-the-ground Jean Michel Frank–style sofas make the ceiling seem higher and the space more loftlike. Leather wing chairs are intentionally mismatched, which helps keep the living room from seeming uptight or stuffy. The six-foot-square coffee table is a rich English teal that's the color of a 1960s Bentley. The folding metal campaign chair is a nineteenth-century cousin of the metamorphic chair at the other end of the room. Celebrated English equestrian artist Sir Alfred Munnings created the paintings over the eighteenth-century American mantel.

We designed the ash table for the dining room and surrounded it with Wiener Werkstätte chairs. The paneled walls are painted a highly reflective white. Echoing the striped dhurrie in the living room is a diamond-and-stripe-patterned rug. Tall white plaster urns were bought at Conran's. OPPOSITE: The owner considers the kitchen the most important room in the house, and the loft theme was continued by adding a pressed tin ceiling and moldings, using stainless steel for the open shelves, cabinets, and countertops.

FOLK ART

FALDO
The Living Room
DIAMOND & BARATTA

FOLK ART HAS HAD A PROFOUND effect on our work. We admire decorative objects made by artisans and craftsmen with little or no formal training, and they often inspire us to create new works — murals, lamps, chairs, rugs — with the same naive or primitive spirit. As much as we enjoy creating new heirlooms, it is more of a privilege to work with genuine artifacts.

One of our clients decided to purchase a historic Greenwich Village town house because it would be the appropriate backdrop for her fabulous folk-art collection, which we helped her amass for her previous apartment. Without turning the Federal house into a museum, we wanted to pay tribute to historic American style, which is understated, unpretentious, and optimistic. It was also important that the decorating not overwhelm the antiques and paintings, which are exquisite but not grand — we had to keep our eyes on the prize.

Purists might quibble with how we furnished the rooms, but our client was thrilled because she's able to live comfortably and happily among her collections.

OPPOSITE: We museum-mounted a six-foot-tall antique shop sign. THIS PAGE: In the sitting room an antique barber's sign is juxtaposed with an early-nineteenth-century portrait on a wall covered in rich red felt that has more clarity and depth than a painted wall. The coffee table is a Pennsylvania Dutch trunk. We designed the sofa's plaid fabric — a custom weave of chocolate, red, taupe, and steel blue — to complement the objets d'art. The tartan rug uses the same colors but in reverse proportions, for a yin-yang effect.

BARBER SHOP

AMERICAN PHOTOGRAPHS

THE TIMES ATLAS COMPREHENSIVE EDITION   HOUGHTON MIFFLIN COMPANY

Historical Atlas of the United States

One of the owner's rare and fragile early American fireman's parade hats sits on the arm of a sofa upholstered in custom-colored wool tartan that we had woven in Scotland by a firm that makes fabrics for kilts. OPPOSITE: We designed special brackets to display the collection of firemen's hats. Arches were added to give the awkwardly shaped family room better proportions and to showcase the hats. The hooked rug has images of nineteenth-century firehouses, and the coffee-table trunk features a carved American eagle on one side and the words "E Pluribus Unum."

PRECEDING PAGE: In the living room the swags and jabots were inspired by draperies we saw at the historic Schuyler Mansion in Albany, New York. Because this room faces north, the walls were painted yellow to create a sunny feeling. The antique Chippendale sofa is upholstered with a Scotch ingrain pictorial weave of eighteenth-century houses. The needlepoint rug was based on a coverlet we saw at Historic Deerfield, a museum community in western Massachusetts devoted to preservation. All of the paintings in this room are folk-art portraits.
THIS PAGE: The chimney breast above the fireplace was designed specifically to display the magnificent museum-quality album quilt. Animals from Noah's ark parade across the mantel. The wing chair is upholstered in a historic toile. The pillows on the sofa are made from antique crocheted buggy blankets, and the enormous jug by the fireplace is nineteenth-century Staffordshire.

We consider the chocolate-brown needlepoint rug contemporary folk art; we based it on early American theorem paintings, which were usually done on velvet by young girls using layers of stencils to create a decorative effect. Pale pink linen covers the walls. The shades are made from handwoven fabric trimmed with custom-woven tape, and the lolling chair and wing chair are covered in the same material. The nineteenth-century tiger-maple four-poster bed has a crocheted canopy. The owner collected the many wonderful antique quilts that are piled at the foot of the bed. The nineteenth-century portrait is unusual because it shows a man wearing sunglasses.

OUR INFATUATION WITH FOLK ART IS shared by many of our clients. Like us, they appreciate naive artistry, unexpected whimsy, and objects with quirky histories. It is especially appealing in brand-new houses, imbuing them with a sense of history, charm, and character. We are often asked to create hybrid homes that have both genuine folk art as well as works by contemporary artisans that we consider the folk art of tomorrow, such as the wraparound mural that we commissioned for the living room of a new waterfront house on the North Shore of Long Island. Painted in a primitive American vernacular, it depicts eighteenth-century life on the Gold Coast, placing historic buildings and figures in an accurate geographic context. The mural gives the newly built house instant landmark status.

OPPOSITE: The needlepoint pillow is trimmed with a braid from an artisan who makes all our braided rugs.
THIS PAGE: The sofa is upholstered in a handwoven, sea-blue glen plaid.

There is something transcendent about the sky, water, and trees on a well-painted mural that acts like a window, transporting you outside. This is a contemporary artist's version of what the North Shore of Long Island would have looked like in the eighteenth century (detail on p. 67). Delft tiles not only surround the fireplace but also inspired the design of the needlepoint rug, which features sailing ships and windmills.

OPPOSITE: New and old textiles mix along the staircase. An antique quilt is attached to a custom stretcher that follows the curve of the wall. The rest of the hall is covered in Scotch ingrain wool woven with eighteenth-century houses. **THIS PAGE:** The custom hurricane-style sconces are nearly three feet tall and feature etchings of sailing ships. The ship's-wheel mirror is an antique, and the striped lighthouse is our fantasy.

OPPOSITE: We believe that foyers should be as well furnished as any other room in a house. This one has a runner based on traditional wool-work floral appliqués.

THIS PAGE: An early-American quilt inspired the dining-room rug. The walls are hand stenciled with pineapples, eagles, and baskets of flowers. We used 1920s floral wallpaper to make lamp shades for the chandelier. One of the dining-room chairs is an antique, and the rest are our copies; we had monochromatic pears, apples, and berries embroidered onto the plaid fabric that covers their backs and seats.

An antique hooked rug hangs over the tiger-maple bed that is dressed with matelassé linens embroidered with flowers. The pattern for the needlepoint rug came from an antique embroidered coverlet. A tiny leaf-and-flower Bennison fabric that gives a sense of texture covers the walls. **OPPOSITE:** The view is the main decoration in the master bath. The walls surrounding the tub are stenciled with flowers. A braided trim finishes the custom hooked sunflower-and-bumblebee rug.

WHEN CLIENTS OF OURS IN NEW YORK CITY BOUGHT A weekend house in Greenwich, Connecticut, they envisioned a rambling, family-friendly retreat to accommodate the recreational needs of their many children and dogs. Creating an exuberant, colorful playhouse appealed to them as parents and as renegades who wouldn't mind stirring up their conservative neighbors. We devised a whimsical riff on all-American style, a mixture of antiques and folk art set into rooms with happy, saturated colors.

As the scheme for the house developed, we could not find fabrics that had the bold, ebullient character that the living room demanded. We wanted a country gestalt that was fresher, bolder, and brighter than anything we had ever seen. So, for the very first time, we created a custom print, featuring red-and-white roosters on an egg-yolk-yellow ground. It opened our eyes to the power of a single fabric to establish a leitmotif for a home.

A cast-iron dog lolls on the green-and-white hand-painted checkerboard floor in the foyer. The reverse-flag hooked rug was probably made by a freed slave. The antique schoolhouse chair has a writing desk and a drawer underneath for supplies.

In the farmhouse spirit the living-room walls are sunflower yellow. The rooster weather vane on the right side of the room inspired the fabric on the sofas and club chair. Patchwork quilts were commissioned so we could turn them into cushions for the wicker furniture. We framed an antique fire board to hang over the fireplace. This was the first time we had braided rugs made in a target pattern.

Monet's garden at Giverny inspired the colors of the dining room. A weather vane sits between two willow-ware lamps at the far end of the room. The Windsor chairs have cushions and antimacassars made of a handwoven windowpane fabric, and the pair of antique tole chandeliers was purchased at auction.

The kitchen was designed for serious cooking and hanging out. We painted the ceiling sky blue to create a sense of expansiveness and the floors high-gloss enamel French blue. The base of the island was inspired by a design by the great English architect Sir Edwin Lutyens; the top is butcher block. We turned vintage watercoolers into lamps and used flag posters to embellish the shades. The folk-art apple on the wall was once a roadside sign for a ''pick-your-own'' orchard.

When sewn together in an intentionally discordant way, the handwoven runners here look like modern paintings. We designed the bed to resemble an antique. The folk-art painting above it is early twentieth century. The eighteenth-century blanket chest still has its original paint. Enduring affection for the owners' dogs is evident in the weather vane atop the antique pine mantel. Above it an antique louver decorates the gabled soffit.

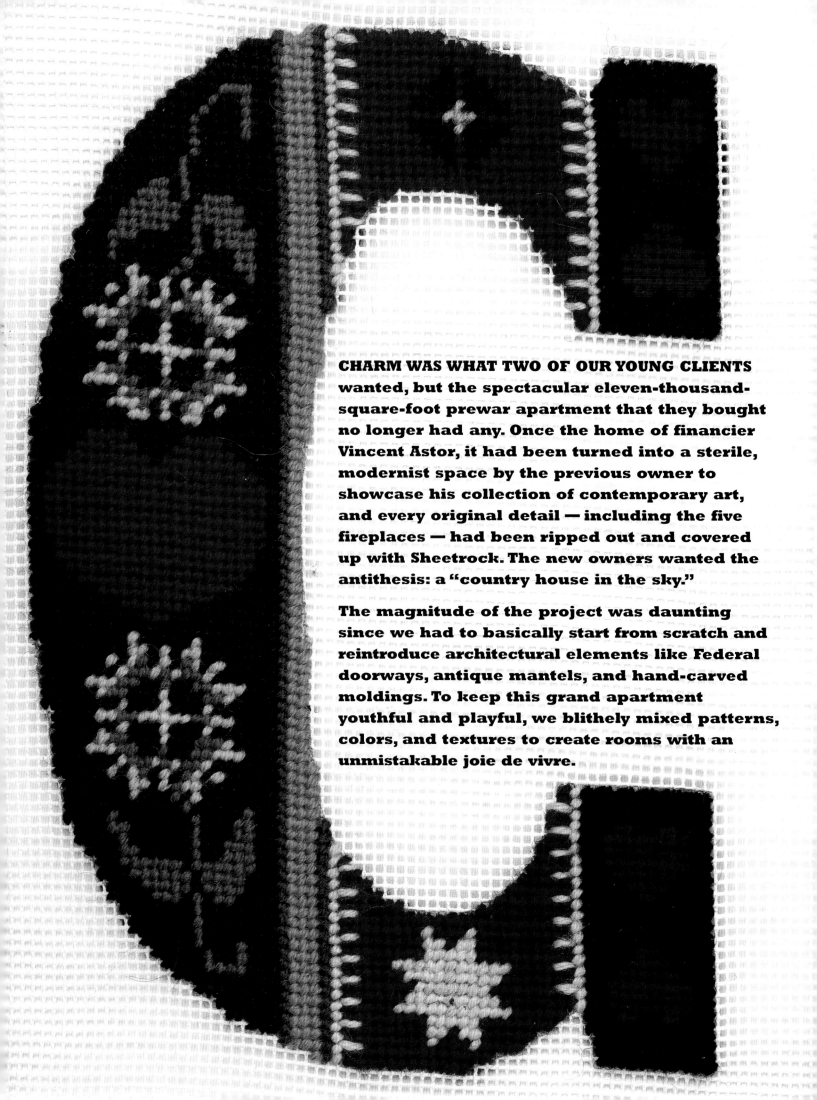

CHARM WAS WHAT TWO OF OUR YOUNG CLIENTS wanted, but the spectacular eleven-thousand-square-foot prewar apartment that they bought no longer had any. Once the home of financier Vincent Astor, it had been turned into a sterile, modernist space by the previous owner to showcase his collection of contemporary art, and every original detail — including the five fireplaces — had been ripped out and covered up with Sheetrock. The new owners wanted the antithesis: a "country house in the sky."

The magnitude of the project was daunting since we had to basically start from scratch and reintroduce architectural elements like Federal doorways, antique mantels, and hand-carved moldings. To keep this grand apartment youthful and playful, we blithely mixed patterns, colors, and textures to create rooms with an unmistakable joie de vivre.

A hand-carved Federal pediment frames the view from the dining room through the breakfast room into the kitchen. The breakfast-room walls are covered in a whimsical blue sunflower fabric.

PRECEDING PAGE LEFT: To make the main hallway's sixty-foot-long braided rug — possibly the world's longest — the New Hampshire woman who braids our rugs had to rent a school gymnasium to work on it. We restored the hall's original vaulted ceiling and added new moldings and pilasters to break up the space and keep it from looking like a hotel lobby.

PRECEDING PAGE RIGHT: The antique English wing chair is upholstered in an ingrain wool with roses. We made the pillows from antique English needlepoints and trimmed them with braided-rug braid.

THIS PAGE: The layering of patterns-on-patterns in the living room is innovative and harmonious because we used a controlled spectrum of color — from the warmest green-blues to the coolest periwinkles — for a calm, monochromatic effect. The walls are covered with a hand-blocked linen from Clarence House. Over the antique American mantel is Jamie Wyeth's *Fog Bound Island*. The wing chair next to the fireplace is upholstered in an antique American quilt.

OPPOSITE: For the sofa we had flowers embroidered onto the handwoven windowpane fabric. The museum-quality quilt hanging on the wall dates from 1869; we bought it at American Hurrah, a pioneering New York folk-art gallery that, alas, no longer exists. THIS PAGE: For the very first time, we combined our two favorite rug styles into one integrated rug, which is one way to update folk-art traditions: hooked medallions, based on delft-tile motifs and botanical prints, are surrounded by braided circles.

The wallpaper in the dining room is Zuber & Cie's historic Views of North America. We designed the cherry table with Spanish-style feet. Needlepointed antimacassars and cushions adorn the antique Windsor chairs, while the wing chairs at either end of the table are upholstered in red felt. The valances were inspired by ones we saw at a historic house, and the sheers are crocheted lace. Antique wallpaper covers the shades on the matching brass chandeliers. A nineteenth-century coverlet, an exquisite folk-art specimen, hangs over the fireplace.

OPPOSITE: The rug reflects the passions of the home owner, who is an accomplished wildlife photographer. We designed the sofa fabric with squirrels, butterflies, and blue jays especially for this room. The draperies are red felted flannel.
THIS PAGE: In the family room a weathered Parcheesi board and scenic hooked rug hang on walls covered with a cozy, over-scale tartan that was laminated for the matching lamp shade.

ONE OF OUR CLIENTS WAS A DEDICATED ANGLOPHILE until she and her husband bought a house in East Hampton, New York, which is one of the most charming, quintessentially American towns on the planet. She decided that she would collect Americana for this home, and because she possesses exceptional taste and unbridled enthusiasm, she asked us to help her find incredible American furniture and accessories. But before we could go shopping, we had to do major construction, for the house was quite plain and lacked romance.

We added double-hung and diamond windows, overhangs, and porches to make it look like a been-there-forever, storybook East Hampton house. We also added a five-thousand-square-foot addition — basically a house behind the house — to blend into the historic neighborhood. It was essential that the house look and feel like a venerable summer cottage. Inside we were very playful, creating a skylit staircase that seems to be leading you outside and into a clapboard-and-shingle lighthouse (but which is actually the guest wing).

Folk-art horses are a dominant presence, for the owners are racing fans, but the owners did not limit themselves to acquiring equine objects. We amassed samplers, framed woollies, spatterware, and iron doorstops and turned everything from vintage roulette wheels to antique coffee grinders into one-of-a-kind folk-art lamps. These stunning artworks are never overwhelming but, rather, create a warm, textured, and colorful background.

This indoor space looks like it is outside: the exterior is meant to resemble a light-house. Upstairs are guest rooms. A collection of framed woollies — needlework done by sailors long ago — lines the staircase.

OPPOSITE: All the architectural details — shutters, windows, over-door pediment, covered porch, and settle — are new but look original.
THIS PAGE: This patrician pine-paneled mudroom was built in England and shipped here for installation. A hooked rug that resembles a patchwork quilt lies on top of a herringbone brick floor. The mini-mural over the settle on the east wall is of East Hampton in the eighteenth century; mini-murals of Montauk and Sag Harbor are on other walls.

Horses are woven into the Scotch ingrain wool that covers the sofa and club chair in the pale sky-blue family room, which links the new and old sections of the house. An antique trunk with its original paint functions as a coffee table. The roulette-wheel lamp is decorated with hand-painted horses; the other lamp is made from an antique spatterware ice chest. **OPPOSITE:** Summer in Saratoga is our name for the hooked-and-braided rug.

A niche off the living room has walls covered in summery Nantucket red linen. The superb circa 1700 William & Mary chest has its original paint. We turned an old leather fire bucket into a lamp with a calico shade. OPPOSITE: An antique pine mantel gives the new family room a sense of history. So do planked walls — and glass doors with oval mullions and Colonial Revival pediments; we hung vintage American hooked rugs above them. The riding-boot lamp was made from an old shop sign.

To hide the acres of Sheetrock in the existing barnlike family room off the kitchen, we covered the walls and ceiling in a blue-green Scottish kilt fabric that has a touch of Nantucket red. The braided rug is red and white. We love the lines of this antique saddle-seat wing chair. The floral Brunschwig & Fils fabric on the sofa and chair are trapunto quilted. Framed samplers hang on the wall. Antique hooked rugs sit atop the rustic mantel.
OPPOSITE: Transforming folk-art pieces into unique table lamps gives a house a sense of history and has become one of our trademarks.

Needlework samplers are classic American folk art, and we collected eighteenth- and nineteenth-century examples for this house. We also created a giant needlepoint sampler rug for the living room.
OPPOSITE: Shelves lined in Nantucket red linen make a stunning backdrop for a collection of blue-and-white English and American spatterware jugs and pitchers. The painted trunk that functions as a coffee table dates to 1776. The large pillow on the sofa was made from an antique New Hampshire quilt top.

This is one of the many eighteenth-century-style gateleg tables that didn't actually exist back then but that we have custom made for clients. **OPPOSITE:** The nineteenth-century cabinet is used to display a collection of painted doorstops. Cotton embroidered in India covers the walls, and the chandelier is nineteenth-century Dutch.

A work of art itself, the plaid trellis porch is based on a porch we saw in Nantucket. The screens are sandwiched between the trellises. The floor is a historic brick herringbone pattern. The antique wicker furniture and new mahogany dining table and chairs are painted the same Copen blue. **FOLLOWING PAGE LEFT:** We added the ship's-wheel-inspired window and then designed the tester of the tiger-maple bed to line up with the mullion. The lamps are made from antique barge-ware teapots. Antique samplers in maple frames hang behind them. **FOLLOWING PAGE RIGHT:** The same hot-air-balloon toile was used for the walls, bedding, curtains, and upholstery in the master bedroom.

Shaker pegs encircle the guest room, which has a Shaker-inspired woodwork sunrise on the wall over the matching full-size antique beds. The down comforters are made from antique quilts embellished with pearl buttons, and the hooked rug is patterned after a quilt.

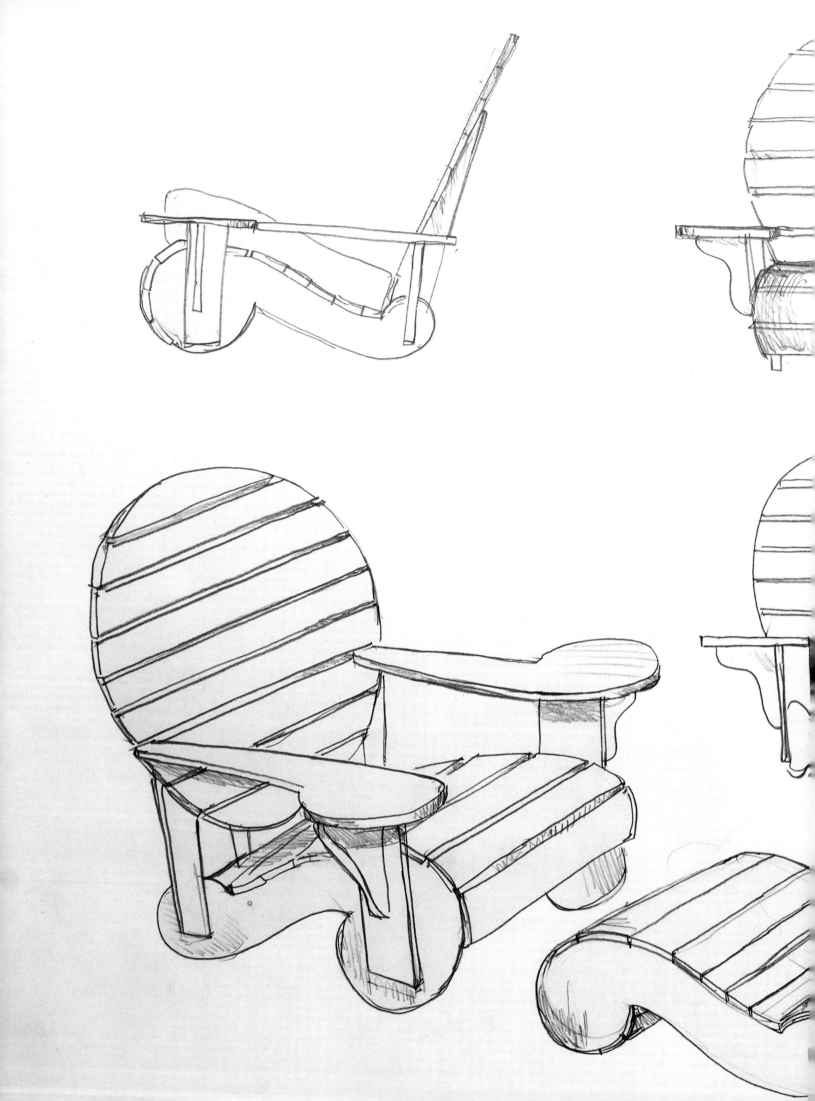

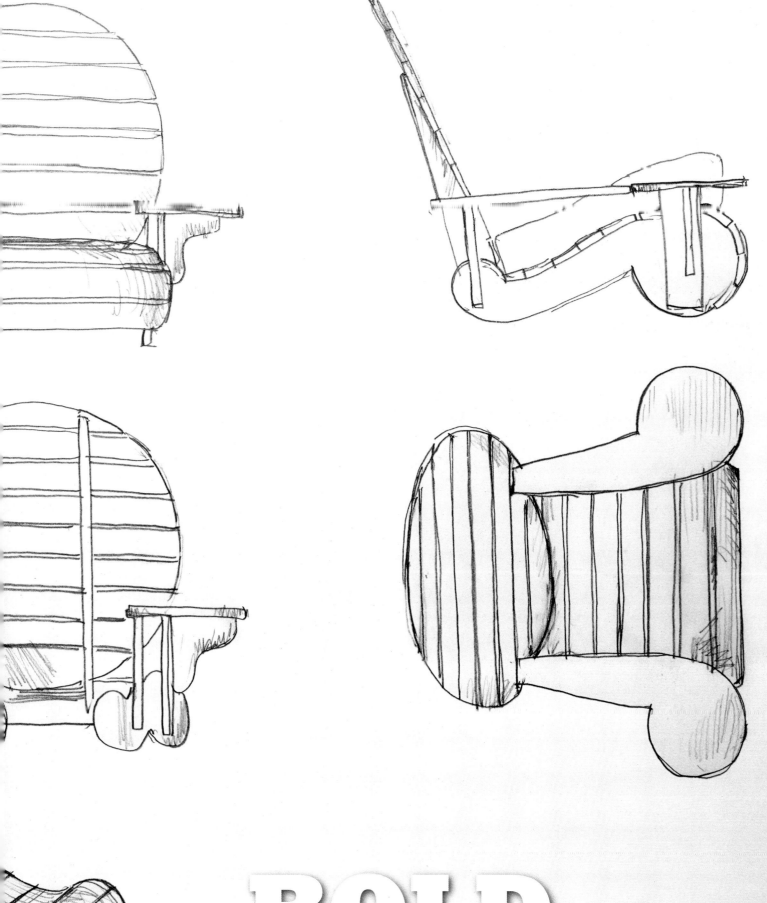
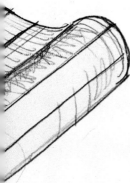

BOLD
THEMES

WHEN THE SO-CALLED BEE HOUSE WAS FIRST PUBLISHED IN *House & Garden*, many people were startled. They knew we liked to play with themes, but they couldn't believe how many bee motifs we'd actually incorporated into one residence. (Truthfully, neither could we.) But we had been lucky: we had a courageous and accommodating client — Tony's sister, who had already let him design her wedding with a bumblebee theme because she and her husband's last names both begin with the letter B. (For their reception we made bee-themed T-shirts that were used to slipcover the rental chairs and were taken home as souvenirs by the guests.) So when they bought a magnificent Victorian house on the New Jersey shore and nicknamed it the Beehive, we knew it was a cue to let our imaginations run wild.

The first thing we designed was the living-room rug, and we based it on a honeycomb; each needlepointed hexagonal component contains a different image, including hives, honeypots, sunflowers, and bumblebees. But what gives this house its sting is the bold use of color. The initial palette was easy to choose — yellow-jacket yellow, black, and white — and then we added copious amounts of turquoise, orange, and green.

As we scoured flea markets and antique stores for appropriate accessories, we discovered we were not alone in our obsession. The clients' friends started buying them bee-themed gifts, such as a "Bee right back" sign that sometimes hangs on the front door. Original, unusual, and over the top, the house is truly a honeypot.

A collection of vintage skeps — the conical braided straw hives of yesteryear — adorn a marble-topped American crotch-mahogany table.

Before decorating, we made architectural revisions, lining up the doorways of the foyer, living room, and library to create an enfilade. The repetition of colors and patterns helps link the three distinct spaces, as does the high-gloss black floor that makes the colors pop. Turquoise grosgrain ribbon was used as a trim around the awning-stripe walls. Victorian chairs in the living room were upholstered in antique quilts. The diamond fabric on the sofa and wing chair in the living room is our own wool gingham woven on the diagonal.

The color story was repeated in
new ways on the screened porch.
A black-and-white checkerboard
was painted on the floor. Vintage
rattan furniture was painted black
and topped with turquoise-and-
white-striped cushions and throw
pillows embroidered with bees.
OPPOSITE: The floor of the breakfast room was painted turquoise
and decorated with more bee im-
agery. The valance and shades
were made of a new fabric called
Diamonds and Roses that subse-
quently became part of our Lee
Jofa line. Large-scale gingham
wallpaper covers the ceiling.

HONEY

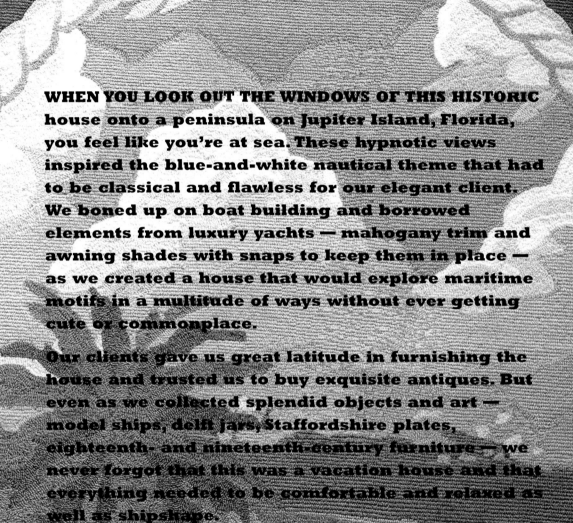

WHEN YOU LOOK OUT THE WINDOWS OF THIS HISTORIC house onto a peninsula on Jupiter Island, Florida, you feel like you're at sea. These hypnotic views inspired the blue-and-white nautical theme that had to be classical and flawless for our elegant client. We boned up on boat building and borrowed elements from luxury yachts — mahogany trim and awning shades with snaps to keep them in place — as we created a house that would explore maritime motifs in a multitude of ways without ever getting cute or commonplace.

Our clients gave us great latitude in furnishing the house and trusted us to buy exquisite antiques. But even as we collected splendid objects and art — model ships, delft jars, Staffordshire plates, eighteenth- and nineteenth-century furniture — we never forgot that this was a vacation house and that everything needed to be comfortable and relaxed as well as shipshape.

Jupiter Inlet Light, Florida

OPPOSITE: Lighthouses from around the world adorn the rug woven for the son's room.
THIS PAGE: On the sofa the center pillow is a needlepoint of a great sailing ship; nautical knots decorate the ends of the bolsters. The diorama on the wall is an antique.

The sun-porch walls are covered in a Bennison cotton stripe from England that is a soft counterpoint to the mahogany trim, shutters, and furniture. The room has five needlepoint rugs trimmed with braid; the three round ones depict sailing ships, and the two square ones feature compasses. The sofas are our version of English Regency in mahogany and cane. Nautical-patterned Staffordshire plates and miniature ship models are displayed in corner cabinets wo designed in tiger maple and mahogany.

PRECEDING PAGE: A folding screen that we commissioned for the house and consider a future heirloom dominates the den. The frame is mahogany, and the original ship paintings are by Ilya Shavel. Fabric that resembles a Chinese fretwork pattern covers the walls. The cotton plaid on the sofa and chair was custom woven. An antique leather captain's trunk serves as the coffee table. The carpet is a rough jute matting. The Chesterfield chair's natural leather ottoman is our version of a gout stool. Small artifacts — a ship in a bottle and a brass alligator — are lighthearted, thematic touches.

THIS PAGE: Flowers are layered with the nautical motif in the living room, whose walls are covered in a clear sky-blue raw silk. The needlepoint rug features bouquets in the palest pinks, yellows, blues, and grays. A basket of flowers was appliquéd onto the ottoman, which is trimmed in ribbon. The legs of the chairs were hand painted with ribbons and flowers. Ships are etched onto the glass sconces above the stone mantelpiece, which is original to the house and dates back to the nineteenth century.

OPPOSITE: The raw Indian silk curtains are trimmed with custom-striped grosgrain ribbons. The settee is upholstered in raw silk, too, with a striped cord and gimp welting.
THIS PAGE: In the dining room the walls are covered in apple-green raw silk, and the sea-blue sconces were custom blown. Antique English knife boxes sit on the eighteenth-century English mahogany sideboard, which has intricate anchor-and-nautical marquetry.

Delft-style images of lighthouses and ships are emblazoned on the needlepoint rug in the dining room. Flower baskets are woven into the Scotch ingrain wool slipcovers trimmed with grosgrain ribbon that adorn the eighteenth-century Chippendale chairs. The raw silk curtains are trimmed with green ribbon. A set of nineteenth-century English Staffordshire festooned with shells and ships hangs on the apple-green walls. Suspended over the table is a pair of three-tiered delft chandeliers.

FOLLOWING PAGE LEFT: In the breakfast room a collection of nineteenth-century Staffordshire pitchers sits on a cherry table with a painted base that we designed. The nineteenth-century English captain's chairs have woven cushions depicting local palm trees and nautical motifs.

We added new etched glass to the antique lantern overhead. The valances are made of a matelassé that we had embroidered with blue thread. Custom-colored ribbons hold together the venetian blinds. Ships' wheels and anchors are embedded in the gingham wallpaper.

FOLLOWING PAGE RIGHT: Sea-green antique Wedgwood is displayed in an oak hutch. On the wall framed antique woollies — needlework done by men at sea — hang above a mahogany chair of our own design with an embroidered medallion.

LIKE SO MANY OLD BEACH HOUSES, THIS ONE HAD LOST much of its charm through neglect (as well as a fire), so we needed to use architecture to create a sense of history and tradition, adding moldings, mantels, bay windows, and glass doors that would seem to have been there forever. Our plan focused on reducing the house down to pure forms and colors, so we had to choose every element with extra care because there would be no extraneous details to divert one's attention. The result is the Platonic ideal of the all-American beach house, a timeless residence that's as simple as it is sumptuous.

While most people assume the red-white-and-blue color theme was chosen for its patriotic connotations, it was actually selected as a backdrop for the owners' first-rate collection of Jean Dubuffet paintings, which ultimately were not hung in the house. Nevertheless, the paintings inspired how we used strong color and shapes to create rooms that are as artful, delightful, and thoughtful as a diorama.

OPPOSITE: The cobalt-blue-and-white quilt is from the 1920s.
THIS PAGE: A wall of windows, painted wood furniture, and awning-stripe shades combine to make the living room look like a porch. The round-back chair and French-curve footrest are our take on classic Adirondack style. The sofa was inspired by one that the legendary decorator Sister Parish used to have on the porch of her house in Maine, and the lighthouse lamp was custom made.

Although we have commissioned hundreds of braided rugs in our career, this one is unique; we call it the cosmic-consciousness rug because the pattern is deliberately random and intended to evoke the constellations. By using the same marine blue throughout the front sitting room, all the furniture looks like sculpture. Painted white and upholstered in wide stripes, the Victorian chairs assume a modern attitude.

The dining room (which had been the living room
before we renovated the house) is what we call American
Minimalism — using the vocabulary of country decorating in a modern way. All of the floors and new architectural details are painted a glossy white. In this setting
the innate elegance of every object — the Windsor chairs
and bench, the cut-out trestle table, the antique lantern,
the eglomise mirror over the fireplace — is unmistakable.

OPPOSITE: The floors were painted with cobalt-blue-and-black Dalmatian spots; an artisan used an eye-dropper filled with paint to create the effect. Blue-and-white tattersall handkerchief linen curtains decorate the glass doors of the kitchen cupboards. The captain's chairs came from an old Masonic Lodge, and the oilcloth-covered table is a wink to farmhouse style and simpler times. The porcelain ceiling fixtures are contemporary Italian.

THIS PAGE: A quintessential feature of old country houses is the back staircase, and this one is as spiffy as they come with its gingham wall-papered walls and woven checker-board runner. The interior door with a mullion pattern around a clear middle comes from a turn-of-the-century Hamptons house and creates an echo of patterns.

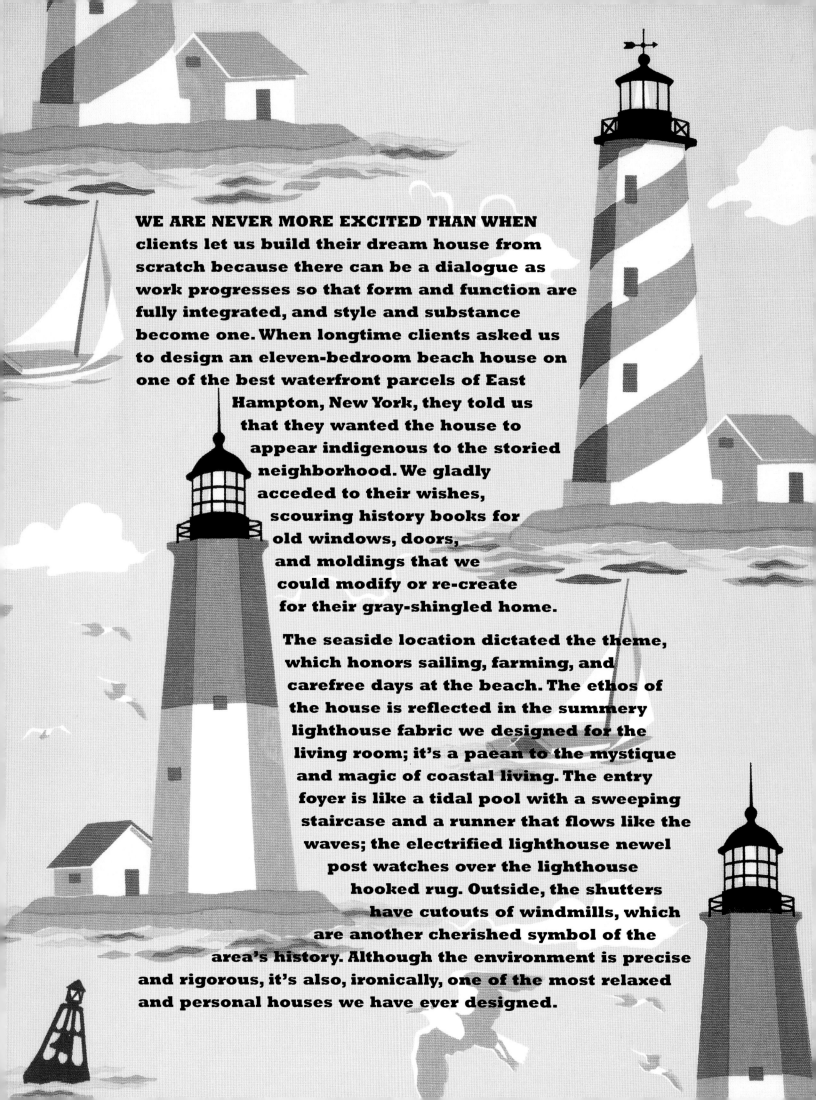

WE ARE NEVER MORE EXCITED THAN WHEN clients let us build their dream house from scratch because there can be a dialogue as work progresses so that form and function are fully integrated, and style and substance become one. When longtime clients asked us to design an eleven-bedroom beach house on one of the best waterfront parcels of East Hampton, New York, they told us that they wanted the house to appear indigenous to the storied neighborhood. We gladly acceded to their wishes, scouring history books for old windows, doors, and moldings that we could modify or re-create for their gray-shingled home.

The seaside location dictated the theme, which honors sailing, farming, and carefree days at the beach. The ethos of the house is reflected in the summery lighthouse fabric we designed for the living room; it's a paean to the mystique and magic of coastal living. The entry foyer is like a tidal pool with a sweeping staircase and a runner that flows like the waves; the electrified lighthouse newel post watches over the lighthouse hooked rug. Outside, the shutters have cutouts of windmills, which are another cherished symbol of the area's history. Although the environment is precise and rigorous, it's also, ironically, one of the most relaxed and personal houses we have ever designed.

OPPOSITE: Detail of our lighthouses
fabric that we did for Lee Jofa.
THIS PAGE: From the moment guests
enter the foyer, they are aware that this
house celebrates the distinctive beauty,
joy, and colors of seaside living.

The bright three-story-high living room is topped by a cupola. Motorized shades that disappear into the woodwork allow the owners to modulate the light. The points on the compass rug are accurate. We cut up old quilts for the throw pillows on the white painted chairs, and the sofa is upholstered in a lighthouse fabric we designed. The delft tiles surrounding the fireplace feature sailing ships; the andirons are lighthouses, and another pair of Labrador andirons is used as bookends on the shelves. The large painting is of Scotland's famed St. Andrew's golf course, which, incidentally, resembles the surrounding landscape.

OPPOSITE: Antique lanterns are one of our obsessions, and this one is monumental. We put six electrified hurricanes inside and painted the outside with subtle pinstripes. On the Windsor chairs in the dining room, handwoven plaid antimacassars have a sumptuous yet homespun quality. The ceiling and windows evoke a Victorian-era porch.
THIS PAGE: Antique wide-plank floors give the brand-new house provenance. The lighthouse newel post is clad in both clapboard and mahogany, and the carved door frame is meant to recall early-American hearths with their overmantel paintings.

Each one of the antique Hitchcock chairs in the kitchen has a different shape, color, and history. The brackets and posts that frame the china nook, which is lined in old pine, look like they were rescued from a Victorian porch; a collection of antique glass chocolate molds is displayed on the top shelf. The cabinets are made of old barn boards that were painted and cracked to look as if they were a century old. Stainless-steel countertops and backsplash are a practical and modern touch that keeps the room from becoming precious.

OPPOSITE: Maine Scenic is the name of the fabric we designed for the master bedroom; it features seagulls, fishing boats, and the owners' beloved black labs. Every circle on the hooked rugs features the dogs enjoying human activities, such as sunbathing, golfing, and sailing.
THIS PAGE: An antique quilt covers the tiger-maple bed that we designed. Turn-of-the-last-century columns and brackets and an enormous window inspired by a McKim, Mead & White design frame the ocean view.

A collection of weather vanes dominates one wall of the master bath, which was painted to look timeworn. The floor is stark white Thassos marble. The claw-foot tub is an antique, but we painted the outside blue-green. The eighteenth-century chair has Spanish-style feet like the dining room table's, and the towel rack is heated.

OPPOSITE: In a guest room painted pale robin's-egg blue, antique beds are set into a niche with porchlike moldings. The braided rug is yet another variation on one of our favorite floor coverings; here, it is three circles woven together into one.

1784

Shoes and sporting gear are organized in a vintage potting table in the mudroom, which has brick herringbone floors. Plaid wallpaper covers the ceiling. The light fixtures are nineteenth-century coach lanterns. **OPPOSITE:** A staircase off the kitchen is a gallery of country quilts. The oval rug depicts Eastern Long Island with a jaunty border of nautical flags.

MODERN PASTELS

IF THERE'S NOTHING MORE CONVENTIONAL THAN AN apartment in a 1960s high-rise on the beach in Boca Raton, Florida, there is nothing more unconventional than the way Tony Baratta's parents let us decorate it. Situated on the ground floor with garden and ocean views, it has floor-to-ceiling windows that never let you forget you are in sunny Florida. We gave Tony's parents three schemes to choose from — colorful, traditional, or a walk on the wild side — and, surprisingly, they told us to go wild. Taking our cue from Lilly Pulitzer, we decided we would turn Palm Beach style on its ear by creating a modern, switched-on-Florida environment.

Shopping for furniture at antique stores and resale shops between West Palm Beach and Miami, we discovered extraordinarily bold and interesting furniture that you just don't find in other places. We painted it all an antique white to create the proper backdrop for our high-octane pastels — chartreuse green, cyclamen pink, and periwinkle blue. We used these colors to create our first harlequin fabric, which gave an uptight reproduction bergère an effervescent quality.

Now in their seventies, Tony's parents are energized by living in such a youthful and happy home, and they are proud that it was designed by their son and his longtime business partner. As they say in Boca, "The Barattas are *kvelling*."

The apartments' three main colors are featured in the custom harlequin fabric (detail, opposite). To give the banal Sheetrock walls character as well as color, we covered them in chartreuse linen. The periwinkle-blue lamp sits on an ornate iron table that took on a modern character after we painted it white.

This enormous coffee table is an antique opium bed with a cane top; we removed the rails, headboard, and footboard before painting it white. The vintage armchairs are upholstered in chartreuse chenille and trimmed with pewter nail heads. We had candle stands wired to make the floor lamps. The 1950s sunburst mirror is lacquered wood, and the solid throw pillows are linen.

FOLLOWING PAGE: Austrian architect and designer Josef Frank's exuberant, whimsical, and enchanting Hawaii linen fabric from the 1940s sets the tone for the entire apartment. Still made in Sweden by Svensk Tenn, it has a repeat of 180 centimeters, allowing us to cover the long *lit de repose* (a traditional French "resting bed") so that motifs never appear more than twice. The draperies are made from a custom periwinkle-blue-and-white stripe.

THE ART OF BREAKING GLASS   MATTHEW HALL

TESS GERRITSEN THE SURGEON

OPPOSITE: The bedrooms are not as brazen as they appear here because only one wall is covered in colorful linen; the other three walls are white. The master bedroom is fresh, clear sunflower yellow, Tony's mother's favorite hue. The yellow-and-hot-pink windowpane fabric on the bed was custom woven.

THIS PAGE: Although it is pink this guest room is ironically nicknamed "the boys' room" because it's where the Barattas' four sons stay when they visit. The elaborately carved bed was gilded before we painted it white. The standing lamp is one we designed for the Eden Roc Hotel in Miami Beach, and the night table is a carved Indian bracket that we painted.

171

WHEN ONE OF OUR CLIENTS WAS BUYING AN UNDER-construction house in a gated community on Long Island, she told us that she wanted the interior to have the ambience of a summer garden. To make sure we understood precisely what she meant, she showed us photographs of floral bouquets and blooms that she loved. It was the romantic palette of the flowers that made us wonder if we could push a pastel spectrum into a Pop Art idiom (which usually relies on Day-Glo or primary colors).

Of course our inspiration was Andy Warhol, which led us to enlarge flowers and turn them into graphic, iconic images. By taking conventional forms and reinterpreting them, we managed to revitalize the concept of the traditional flower-filled living room, making it fresh and new.

The scene-setting needlepoint rug is one of the most difficult ones we've ever produced: it required painstaking research to make sure all the flowers were botanically correct and intense coordination to translate a palette of thirty colors into a syncopated grid. It was well worth the effort, for you feel as if you're dreaming and walking on a bed of animated flowers. The rugs in the foyer, with their aerial view of formal French gardens, are equally magical. Like the one in the living room, they are twenty-first-century Pop Art tapestries that could also have hung on the walls.

The foyer establishes the botanical theme, with its grass-green doors, chartreuse walls and upholstery, and chimerical rugs depicting aerial views of formal French gardens.

In the break-the-rules Pop Art spirit, we cut up a Brunschwig & Fils tulip fabric and patch-worked it with a checkerboard of pastel solids to upholster the sofa. The enormous white porcelain urn lamps have yellow-and-white gingham shades. Motorized shades that disappear into the woodwork allow the sun to shine in through unadorned windows and doors. The coffee table is antique Chinese.

The colors in the living room are clear and refreshing. The apricot ottoman, the lemon-yellow fireplace, and the lime, pink, and white plaid on the sofa combine to create a perennial sunny day. The walls are yellow horizontal planking. Jean Lowe created the painting and frame over the mantel.
OPPOSITE: All of the flowers on the needlepoint rug — such as the rose with rose hips, the rubrum lily, and the sunflower — are based on botanical drawings.

OPPOSITE: An eye-catching painting by Lois Dodd hangs on yellow plank walls in the dining room. Orkney Isle chairs, with cushions made of apple-green striped fabric trimmed with grosgrain ribbon, surround a table made of bleached ash.

THIS PAGE: We designed the kitchen island with bookshelves because it can be seen from the living room. The ceilings are covered with gingham wallpaper. Tiles in custom colors — yellow, apple green, chartreuse, apricot, and two pinks — create a jazzy, prismatic backsplash.

We reinvigorated traditional eighteenth-century Chinese-style wallpaper featuring birds, butterflies, and branches by having it painted with a sunflower-yellow background and hot pink peonies. The headboard, comforter, and pillows are chartreuse and white gingham. The carpeting is a chartreuse plaid laid on the diagonal. Pediments hide the mechanics for the motorized venetian blinds.
OPPOSITE: The bathroom walls are chartreuse green reverse-painted glass. Snow-white Thassos marble surrounds the tub. The monogrammed chair is upholstered in terry cloth.

IF THIS COUPLE COULD, THEY WOULD HAVE A WEEKEND HOUSE ON the island of Nantucket, their all-time favorite place on earth. But since these women live and work in Manhattan, they decided that a getaway on the eastern end of Long Island was more practical and convenient. Since we are close friends, they asked our advice before purchasing this house, and we gave it our approval because it had good bones and a cliffside setting with a stunning view of the bay. These factors helped us in creating a Nantucket fantasy for them.

What's more, the owners are unreconstructed preppies and love to dress in Ivy League pinks and greens, so they insisted that the decor also have an unmistakably preppy complexion. The result is a feminine take on nautical style, which we achieved by using pastels that pack a punch. Even on a bleak winter's day, it's the most summery, carefree, and cheerful house imaginable, which makes it the next best thing to a house on Nantucket itself.

OPPOSITE: The entry foyer's hooked rug combines beautiful pastel colors with nautical Nantucket motifs.
THIS PAGE: Victorian furniture painted high-gloss white is upholstered in awning fabric trimmed with watermelon-pink grosgrain ribbon. The carved plant stand is nineteenth century Anglo-Indian that we painted white.

In the living room an antique quilt hangs on a wall painted a sassy sky blue. The sofa is covered in stark white glazed chintz with pink roses and geraniums and yellow-and-red tulips. The custom scalloped Chippendale-style coffee table has blue pinstriped detailing and a top of delft flower tiles (the straw basket of lush hydrangea, peonies, spirea, and white lilacs was arranged by Bill). On the end tables faux-delft tole lamps illuminate splendid pieces of pink lusterware.

NANTUCKET ISLAND
ROBERT GAMBEE

HAMPTONS ASSOULINE

LONG ISLAND A NEWSDAY BOOK ABRAMS

Picturing Nantucket NHA

RAND McNALLY America

The mural in the entry foyer provides the owners a misty view of their beloved Nantucket. The white Windsor bench has a pink pinstripe and a cushion made from a custom-woven Home Sweet Home fabric. **OPPOSITE:** The view from the foyer into the dining room is framed by blue-and-white-striped curtains that also line the pink-and-blue-striped curtains beyond. The pink-and-white rag rug, monogrammed pink slipcovers with dressmaker details, and pink-and-blue fabric walls combine to give the dining room a year-round, rosy sunset glow.

We always fantasized about hanging model boats on wainscoting, and here we finally got our chance. In the family room off the kitchen, we designed special metal supports to hold the owners' collection of vintage pond yachts; we had new sails made for all the boats so that they'd be uniformly white. There's no such thing as pink tartan in Scotland, but that didn't stop us from having a chunky pink tartan rug hand woven for us in Guatemala. One of the owners' mothers made the needlepoint pillows that depict Nantucket scenes. The owners' extensive collection of cast-iron "Old Salt" doorstops and banks are displayed on tables throughout the room.

The pastel needlepoint rug in the
library has a maritime theme with
waves creating the grid and nautical flags
at the intersections.
OPPOSITE: The upholstery fabric looks like preppy
madras, but it's actually a wool tartan that's been recol-
ored and resized and woven for us in Scotland. Blue and
white tiles were laid in a checkerboard around the fireplace, which has lighthouse andirons. The coffee table is an
antique camphor-wood trunk.

OPPOSITE: In the kitchen periwinkle-blue floors are stenciled with whales, mermaids, and ships. We added the diamond windows for a storybook effect. **THIS PAGE:** For the floor of the master bathroom, we had ceramic tiles laid in a pattern to look like gingham, and we designed a custom typeface for the monogram on the towels. Antique dioramas hang on the wainscoting.

LOCATED IN ONE OF MASSACHUSETTS' OLDEST COLONIAL TOWNS, THIS HOUSE is one of the newest, and its acres of bland Sheetrock walls needed to be covered deftly in order to transform it into the ultimate country home. We knew this residence had to be very American, but it also had to be utterly original.

The owners wanted the interiors to be extremely personal, and they encouraged us to create custom furniture and textiles just for them. They also wanted it to be the archetypal family home with a fun-loving vibe and the ambience of a cozy cottage. The wife loves traditional country decorating, especially hearts and flowers, so we incorporated them into the rooms in various ways, using potent pastels to maintain a vivacious, contemporary spirit. The clearest blues, yellows, and pinks appear in nearly every room for a prevailing color scheme that is snappy, upbeat, and melodious.

OPPOSITE: Historic Boston Harbor is depicted in the Scotch ingrain pictorial weave that we designed for the walls in the main hall.
THIS PAGE: Our first — and biggest — challenge was the foyer. We won the job after telling the clients how we planned to re-build the staircase so we could fur-nish the space with a settee upholstered with a twentieth-century quilt top, gigantic lanterns, and a tiger-maple rent table.

PRECEDING PAGE: We commissioned patchwork quilts that incorporate seventeenth-century botanicals with diamonds made of blue, pink, and yellow checked and plaid fabrics; we then turned them into curtains and upholstery. Our eighteenth-century-style bird's-eye maple wing chairs have claw and ball feet; they are upholstered in a pink-and-white herringbone and embellished with a band of hearts made of nail heads. The shelves hold a major collection of pink lusterware featuring ships. We collected antique gold-and-black picture frames as well as antique bird and botanical prints for inspiration to design the needlepoint rug that's a virtual vernissage.

OPPOSITE: All of the tables in the living room, such as the wedding trunk used as a coffee table, are extraordinary examples of wood marquetry; because the husband is not fond of antiques, we made sure every piece was well polished and gleaming.

THIS PAGE: The walls are covered in a bright yellow linen to mask the Sheetrock. The fabric on the winged settee has hand-embroidered flowers, and the contours of the pink wing chair are both distinctive and amusing.

We added mahogany moldings, doors, and trim to give the dining room a classic character. The tiger-maple chairs are covered in two of our woven fabrics for Lee Jofa that mimic bargello. The rug is a giant needlepoint sampler featuring ships, stags, anchors, and silhouettes. **OPPOSITE:** We put together a collection of Staffordshire pitchers to display on a custom tiger-maple dumbwaiter.

A traditional Pennsylvania Dutch hex sign is painted on the floor of the round breakfast room. We designed shelves above and between the windows to display a collection of nineteenth-century ceramic hens. The chandelier is a reproduction of a conservatory planter. **OPPOSITE:** A Hawaiian patchwork quilt inspired the pastel pink, blue, green, and yellow tiles on the backsplash. Two different yellow and white ginghams cover the ceiling and cabinet doors.

OPPOSITE: To give the sunroom an indoor-outdoor feel, we designed elaborate trelliswork with an oval bouquet medallion. The mahogany-and-cane chairs are our overscaled version of Hepplewhite, with cushions of quilted-and-monogrammed pink linen. Hearts decorate the end table.

THIS PAGE: The owners' initials are carved into the headboard of the tiger-maple bed that is dressed with hearts-and-flowers linens from D. Porthault and set into a cove of hot pink linen. The yellow walls are decorated with pink, blue, and white early-American stencils.

FOLLOWING PAGE: After convincing our clients that the natural wood beams and trim should be painted white, we covered the pool pavilion's walls with all-weather awning-stripe fabric and then commissioned an artist to paint nine murals of swimming scenes on the coved ceiling. We also installed nickel-plated lanterns over the pool. We designed the rattan furniture with extrawide mahogany arms so they could hold food and drink. The custom pillows are based on nautical flags and beach balls.

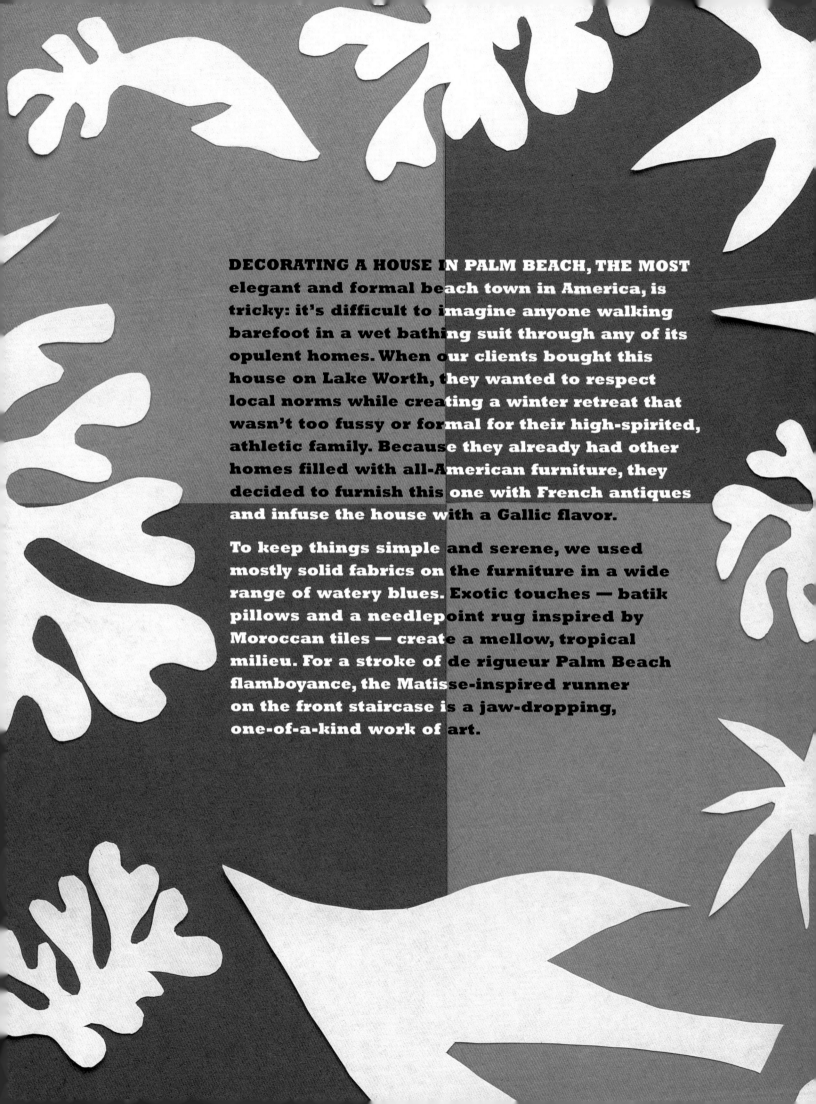

DECORATING A HOUSE IN PALM BEACH, THE MOST
elegant and formal beach town in America, is
tricky: it's difficult to imagine anyone walking
barefoot in a wet bathing suit through any of its
opulent homes. When our clients bought this
house on Lake Worth, they wanted to respect
local norms while creating a winter retreat that
wasn't too fussy or formal for their high-spirited,
athletic family. Because they already had other
homes filled with all-American furniture, they
decided to furnish this one with French antiques
and infuse the house with a Gallic flavor.

To keep things simple and serene, we used
mostly solid fabrics on the furniture in a wide
range of watery blues. Exotic touches — batik
pillows and a needlepoint rug inspired by
Moroccan tiles — create a mellow, tropical
milieu. For a stroke of de rigueur Palm Beach
flamboyance, the Matisse-inspired runner
on the front staircase is a jaw-dropping,
one-of-a-kind work of art.

The runner (detail, opposite) is based on Matisse paper cutouts. Iron banisters evoke French houses; this one was designed to resemble waves. The eighteenth-century French armoire, with its original paint, grazes the ceiling.

On the landing, frosted glass doors in a diamond pattern lead to the master suite. We found the antique lantern in London. **OPPOSITE:** With its walls covered in blue planking and trimmed in white, the living room feels like a luxuriously converted French barn. The fifty-foot-long needlepoint rug in periwinkle and aqua is an homage to Moroccan tiles.

The monochromatic living room is cool and soothing on a sunny day. The throw pillows are hand-dyed batiks from Southeast Asia. The Venetian settee is upholstered in tiny aqua-and-white check. We designed the six-foot-square lacquered coffee table as well as the seven-foot round one on the other side of the room.

FOLLOWING PAGE LEFT: In the dining room a pair of eighteenth-century French corner cabinets stands against walls covered in an aquamarine linen. The antique table has a parquet de Versailles top. Our version of Louis XIV dining chairs has a chipped-paint finish and nail-head trim. The solid aqua braided rug has a black-and-white border.

FOLLOWING PAGE RIGHT: To give the kitchen an old-world aura, we covered the walls in white subway tiles. A magnificent pair of nineteenth-century armoire doors hides the pantry. The inside of the light fixtures is aqua to maintain the blue scheme.

THE NEW TRADITIONALS

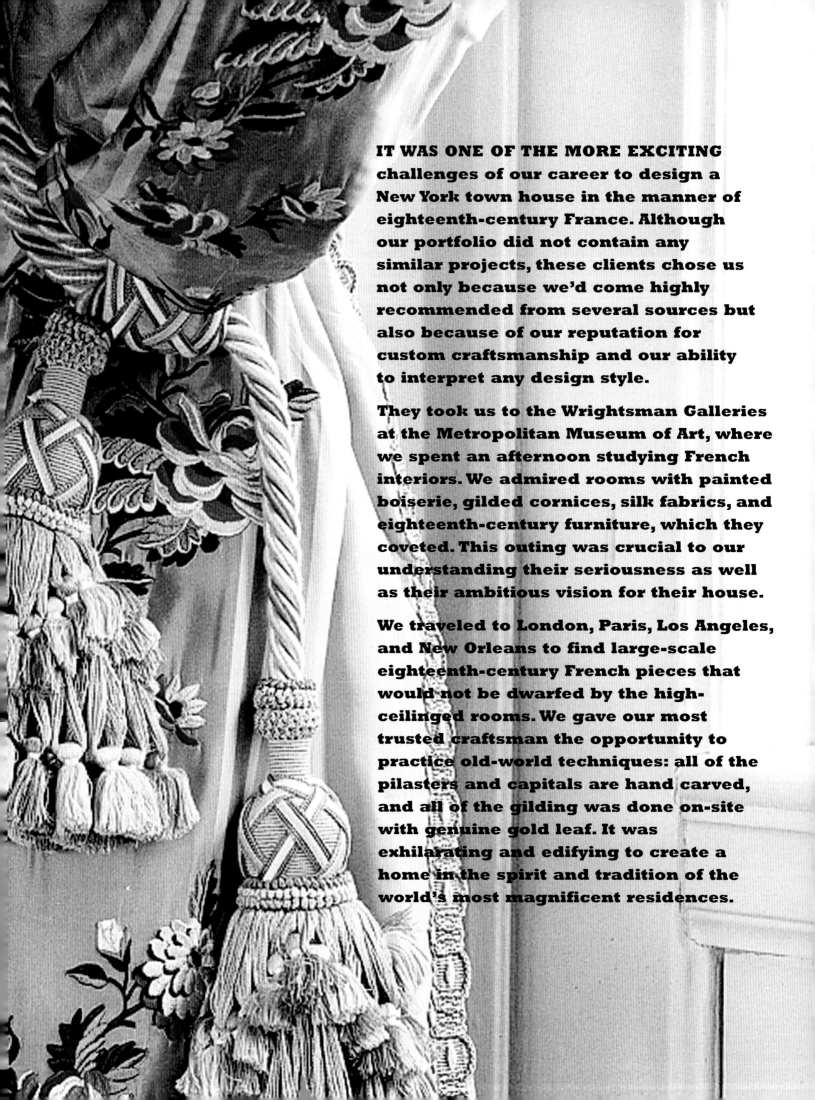

IT WAS ONE OF THE MORE EXCITING challenges of our career to design a New York town house in the manner of eighteenth-century France. Although our portfolio did not contain any similar projects, these clients chose us not only because we'd come highly recommended from several sources but also because of our reputation for custom craftsmanship and our ability to interpret any design style.

They took us to the Wrightsman Galleries at the Metropolitan Museum of Art, where we spent an afternoon studying French interiors. We admired rooms with painted boiserie, gilded cornices, silk fabrics, and eighteenth-century furniture, which they coveted. This outing was crucial to our understanding their seriousness as well as their ambitious vision for their house.

We traveled to London, Paris, Los Angeles, and New Orleans to find large-scale eighteenth-century French pieces that would not be dwarfed by the high-ceilinged rooms. We gave our most trusted craftsman the opportunity to practice old-world techniques: all of the pilasters and capitals are hand carved, and all of the gilding was done on-site with genuine gold leaf. It was exhilarating and edifying to create a home in the spirit and tradition of the world's most magnificent residences.

OPPOSITE: These silk curtains are hand embroidered with flowers and tied back with elaborate silk passementerie.
THIS PAGE: All six stories of the staircase are lined with hand-painted Chinese wallpaper. We worked with Gracie, the venerable wallpaper company, to design the paper so that every tree, bird, and jardinière would be properly placed when it was hung. The faux marquetry floors are hand stenciled.

OPPOSITE: One of two Chinese export jars sits on top of a gilt-and-gesso stand that is also part of a pair. **THIS PAGE:** The salon was a Sheetrock box before we added hand-carved boiserie trimmed with gold leaf. An arched, mirrored niche gives the room a sense of depth and frames the eighteenth-century enamel-and-gilt clock. The gilt settee is upholstered in salmon-colored bouffant velvet with silk damask pillows. The rug is a nineteenth-century Louis Phillipe Aubusson, and the lamps are enormous rose mandarin jars.

We found this nineteenth-century desk with an inlaid clock in New Orleans. The stenciled faux marquetry floor was inspired by one in Catherine the Great's bedroom in St. Petersburg, Russia; it looks absolutely real. Lace sheers cover the windows, and the striped curtains have a trim of embroidered flowers.

OPPOSITE: The bergère is one of four in the living room; all are upholstered in floral silk brocade. The gilt mirror and sconces are eighteenth-century French, as is the console table.

FOLLOWING PAGE LEFT: The vase is painted porcelain.

FOLLOWING PAGE RIGHT: All of the panels in the dining room were hand painted in a nineteenth-century Swedish manner. The chairs are antique lacquered chinoiserie, and the gilt fire screen is nineteenth-century French. The crystal sconces are eighteenth-century English.

OPPOSITE: The coved ceiling and bookshelves in the paneled library are constructed of hand-carved mahogany and crotch-mahogany veneers. To keep the room from becoming too dark, we designed niches for the fireplace and for the sofa, which we covered with blue-green felt. We designed the Aubusson-style rug because we could not find one that had the right combination of colors for the room. The eighteenth-century English wing settee and chairs are upholstered in tapestry. The chandelier is French Empire. THIS PAGE: This antique three-tier book stand is in the style of Robert Adam.

AFTER LIVING IN LONDON AND HONG KONG FOR A decade, our clients and their children returned home to the United States. During their time abroad they had collected modern art, purchased Chinese furniture, and developed an appreciation for classical English style, and they wanted us to incorporate these varied elements into the Italianate house they bought in New Jersey.

Although their house is located in one of those leafy, stately suburbs, they wanted it to be urbane and worldly, so we decided to rethink traditional decorating and push it to the edge of chic. We had a blank canvas on which to work because the house had been completely gutted and had no doors, no floors, and no windows. We used period architecture and sumptuous furnishings to create a cosmopolitan environment that was appropriate for suburban family life.

As we often do, we designed custom needlepoint rugs to set the mood. These have graphic, Chinese fretwork patterns, which are both modern and classic at the same time — the ideal leitmotif for a house whose sensibility bridges continents as well as centuries.

OPPOSITE: Hand embroidery
(detail shown) decorates the
daybeds in the entry foyer.
THIS PAGE: The view into the
living room is framed by a
classic English pediment that
references a pagoda.

The entry foyer has an international flavor: the hand-painted wallpaper is Chinese, the secretary with the clock is Swedish, the Biedermeier table is Austrian, the lantern with lion's heads is English, and the daybeds are French — one is an original, and one is our clone — and they are upholstered in silk ottoman cloth embellished with hand embroidery. The floors are stenciled faux marquetry.

FOLLOWING PAGE: Zen motifs punctuate the eggplant-and-white fretwork-patterned rug. The Art Deco, silver-leafed bergères are upholstered in silk damask whose fronts are hand embroidered to emphasize the fabric's pattern. Pagoda-inspired valances and white silk curtains are hand embroidered with a Chinese fretwork design. The lamps are eighteenth-century Chinese jars with pagoda lamp shades and the coffee table is an antique bed.

The living-room walls are painted a rich, high-gloss aubergine lacquer; we added the white chair rail and dado to keep the room from becoming too dark. The Warhol silk screens really pop on the shiny walls, giving the traditional decor a touch of the avant-garde. The nineteenth-century coffee table is inlaid with mother-of-pearl. The pattern on the damask pillows is embroidered to highlight the design.

The dining-room rug has an egg-
plant hexagon fretwork pattern and
depicts Chinese precious objects.
Gauffrage velvet covers the walls.
Velvet pagoda-style valances are
hand embroidered with Chinese
peonies; the curtains are blue silk
taffeta. In front of the French doors
stand two porcelain pagodas found
in London. The table is an English
antique, as is the chandelier.

A single curtain rod circles the Garden Room, which has French doors on three sides and linen draperies with a custom Greek key border. A late-nineteenth-century opium bed dominates one end of the room. "Delhi Deco" is the nickname we gave to the mahogany furniture because Sir Edwin Lutyens originally designed it for a client in India. Cotton hand printed with eighteenth-century Chinese motifs covers the cushions. The pagoda-style lanterns were made in London.

OPPOSITE: An oval entry hall with eighteenth-century-style Chinese wallpaper leads to the master suite. The hand-stenciled floors look like marquetry.

THIS PAGE: The master suite's custom carpet has Chippendale fretwork and Chinese blossoms such as apple, cherry, and dogwood. We designed the French Deco bed that is upholstered with embossed jade velvet. The pattern on the pink-and-white cotton wall covering and drapes is so small that it looks solid from a distance. The furniture in the sitting area is covered in a hand-printed silk that we designed specially for the room.

We searched high and low to assemble the collection of antique aubergine-and-white delft tiles for the backsplash. The clock is antique English.

OPPOSITE: The kitchen floors were hand painted in a toile pattern in aubergine and white. The double-groin vault ceiling was inspired by one at the Sir John Soane's Museum in London. The custom aubergine lanterns look like they came from an old train station. The island is made from antique English pine.

THIS CLIENT LOVES INTERIOR DECORATING AS MUCH AS we do. She enjoys choosing colors, sifting through fabrics, and hunting for antiques. We have done two other houses with her, and she wanted this one to be traditional and extremely pretty. These days pretty seems to be out of fashion, but she and we believe that pretty rooms never go out of style. She asked to see flowers everywhere — on the rugs, on the furniture, on the walls, on the lamps and accessories. She requested cheerful, pleasing colors — blues, pinks, and pale yellows.

Our inspiration was the English country house with its pedigreed layers of patterned fabrics, but we needed to expand and update the formula for this client, who asked us to renovate the existing house and design a large addition. We built her a gutsy, double-height family room with mammoth Palladian windows and tore out the attic to give the master suite a dramatic new ceiling.

She wanted everything in her home — from the eighteenth- and nineteenth-century furniture to the magnificent pieces of Staffordshire — to contribute to a mood of grace, charm, and welcome. When we put all the pieces together, we had an innovative but deferential American interpretation of classic English decorating.

OPPOSITE: The six-panel front door, which has Colonial hardware, is painted Dutch blue. **THIS PAGE:** A custom needlepoint rug with ribbons of cabbage roses in a trellis pattern is our take on English style; it is now part of our line for Stark Carpet. The nineteenth-century Regency settee is painted with flowers.

An eighteenth-century mantel with carved medallions of tiger maple, mahogany, and pine imbues the newly built family room with a sense of history. So do the eighteenth-century horse painting and delft garniture. The plank walls are painted a soft blue-gray, and the needlepoint rug is our design.

OPPOSITE: The sofa and armchair are upholstered in hand-printed cabbage-rose linen. Inspired by Sister Parish's work at the Kennedy White House, the swags and jabots are made from a nineteenth-century document floral and have a hand-scalloped edge. The standing lamps are converted English torches.

PREVIOUS PAGE LEFT: In the breakfast room a nineteenth-century English document wallpaper is visible through the eighteenth-century Welsh dresser. We turned Staffordshire candlesticks into lamps with shades made of Liberty of London calico. The tole spice boxes are early nineteenth century. The table, which is gateleg, is eighteenth-century Georgian.

PREVIOUS PAGE RIGHT: Nothing is more English than layering fabrics, and we used five different patterns in the family room, including a bright pink toile on the wing chair. The lamps are made from Staffordshire urns. A nineteenth-century painted trunk serves as a coffee table.

THIS PAGE: We designed this hand-painted bed specially for the master suite, which has walls covered in hand-blocked Zuber wallpaper with a crisscross grid of ribbons with flowers. The ribbon motif also appears in the custom rug and the linen fabric on the chairs. Over the bed a pelmet is fashioned from white linen and trimmed with antique blue-and-white-striped and floral ribbons. The painted papier-mâché settee is Victorian. Eighteenth-century English chests are used as night tables, and the lamps are nineteenth-century floral porcelain vases.

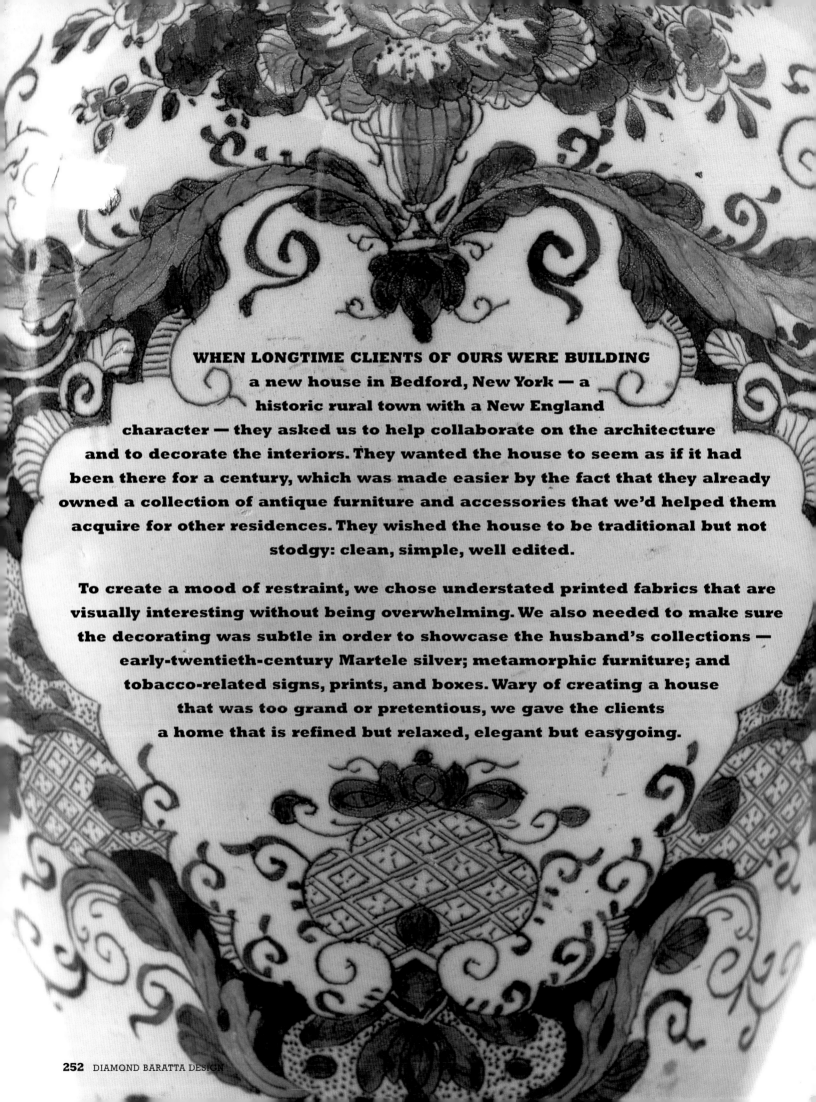

WHEN LONGTIME CLIENTS OF OURS WERE BUILDING
a new house in Bedford, New York — a
historic rural town with a New England
character — they asked us to help collaborate on the architecture
and to decorate the interiors. They wanted the house to seem as if it had
been there for a century, which was made easier by the fact that they already
owned a collection of antique furniture and accessories that we'd helped them
acquire for other residences. They wished the house to be traditional but not
stodgy: clean, simple, well edited.

To create a mood of restraint, we chose understated printed fabrics that are
visually interesting without being overwhelming. We also needed to make sure
the decorating was subtle in order to showcase the husband's collections —
early-twentieth-century Martele silver; metamorphic furniture; and
tobacco-related signs, prints, and boxes. Wary of creating a house
that was too grand or pretentious, we gave the clients
a home that is refined but relaxed, elegant but easygoing.

Blue-gray-green walls and a handwoven straw rug set a serene tone for the living room. We designed the dining room with a glass transom and extrawide pocket doors. The top of the coffee table is a panel taken from an eighteenth-century Coromandel screen we found in Minneapolis. The sofas are upholstered in hand-blocked printed linen. Nail-head swags embellish the taupe suede wing chair.

OPPOSITE: The library and the kitchen are matching octagonal rooms — one on either end of the house. The library's beams and arches are mahogany. A Chesterfield sofa is upholstered in a windowpane plaid, and the Oriental rug is early nineteenth century. The lamp was fashioned from an old cigar-store sign.

THIS PAGE: The kitchen floors are honed bluestone, and antique Staffordshire platters hang on yellow walls trimmed in white. The lanterns are English antiques. The table and Windsor chairs are antique English pine.

OPPOSITE: We designed the potting bench and sink for the greenhouse and installed lanterns in a verdigris finish.
THIS PAGE: The iron table on the screened porch is new but has an antique finish; the top is French lava stone. We commissioned an artist to paint fern botanicals on wood panels with an oil-based paint so they'd withstand the elements, and then we framed them in weatherproof mahogany.

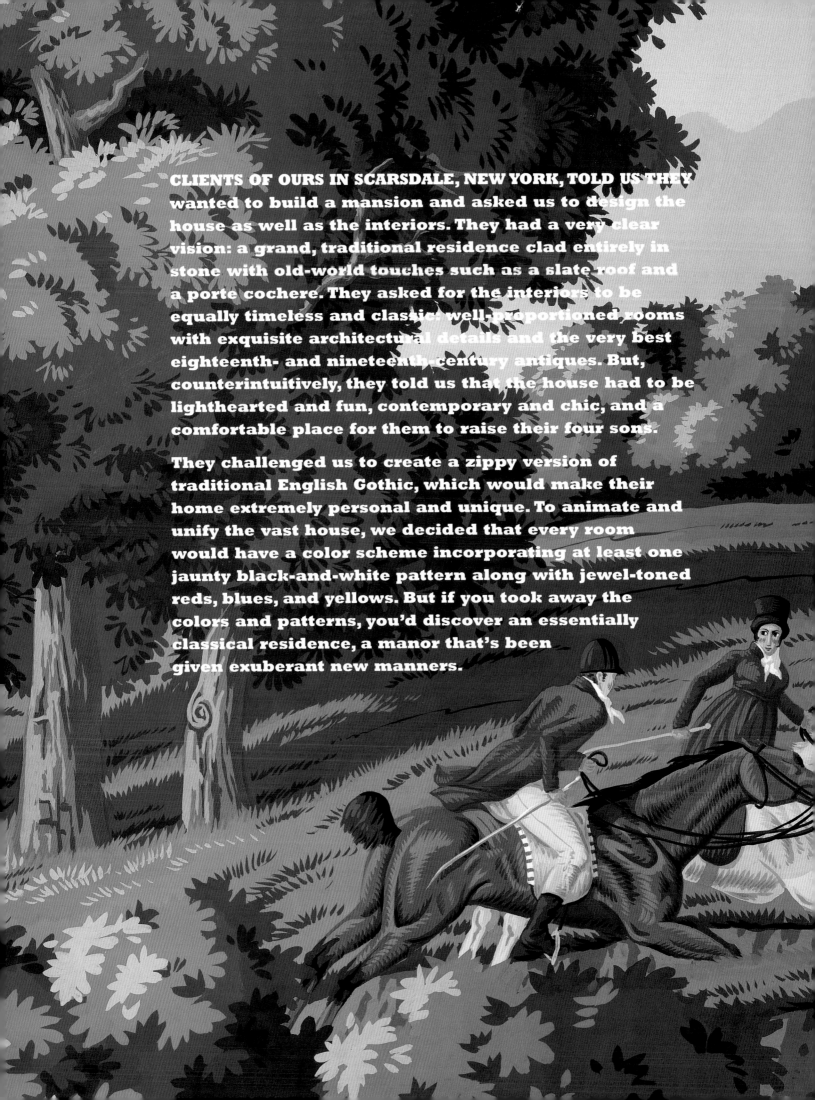

CLIENTS OF OURS IN SCARSDALE, NEW YORK, TOLD US THEY wanted to build a mansion and asked us to design the house as well as the interiors. They had a very clear vision: a grand, traditional residence clad entirely in stone with old-world touches such as a slate roof and a porte cochere. They asked for the interiors to be equally timeless and classic: well-proportioned rooms with exquisite architectural details and the very best eighteenth- and nineteenth-century antiques. But, counterintuitively, they told us that the house had to be lighthearted and fun, contemporary and chic, and a comfortable place for them to raise their four sons.

They challenged us to create a zippy version of traditional English Gothic, which would make their home extremely personal and unique. To animate and unify the vast house, we decided that every room would have a color scheme incorporating at least one jaunty black-and-white pattern along with jewel-toned reds, blues, and yellows. But if you took away the colors and patterns, you'd discover an essentially classical residence, a manor that's been given exuberant new manners.

OPPOSITE: The wallpaper (detail shown here) was painted so the hunters would be riding up the staircase.
THIS PAGE: The crown molding is a series of Gothic arches that frame the hunting-scene wallpaper, which was hand painted in Hong Kong. On the staircase the runner is a custom black-and-white Gothic leaf pattern. The Arts and Crafts Gothic Revival sideboard is museum quality.

PREVIOUS PAGE LEFT: What's black and white and red all over? A custom needlepoint argyle rug. Red felt walls frame a white Gothic arch with a fleur-de-lis that bridges the foyer and family room. The Louis XIV hall chairs are upholstered in a red wool damask.

PREVIOUS PAGE RIGHT: In the billiard room the quatrefoil needlepoint rug, which is based on a historic pattern, looks fresh and modern in black, white, and red. The pool table is mahogany. Heraldic patterns are woven into the fabric on the sofa. High-back chairs are upholstered in cobalt blue felt and decorated with a custom trim embroidered with eight balls. To enhance the color scheme, we had blue glass shades blown for the billiard fixture.

THIS PAGE: Hand-carved panelling in the library is painted a courtly blue-gray. The owners placed the chess pieces where they wanted them when we designed this red-black-and-white chessboard rug. The striped sofa fabric was made exclusively for us at a factory that manufactures silk repp ties. A sumptuous, custom-dyed suede covers the Chesterfield sofa. The king of hearts needlepoint pillow is one of several deck-of-cards pillows — all of them kings — throughout the room. The chandelier is French Empire.

Pocket doors with a glass Gothic arch and carved trefoil lead into the dining room, which has seven windows framed by Regency arches and pilasters. English Regency chairs upholstered in cerulean blue embossed velvet surround the antique table. The "gingham" floor is made of black, white, and gray marble; the kitchen has the same floor.

OPPOSITE: Gothic quatrefoils ring the gray-and-white carved kitchen island. The countertops are blue Bahia granite. Custom heraldic tiles featuring unicorns and lions make up the backsplash. The Gothic glass cabinet doors are inset with cobalt-colored glass diamonds, and Gothic motifs decorate the plaster ceiling. The black-and-white lanterns were made in England.

OPPOSITE: The master suite is enveloped by a crisp black-and-white document toile. Motorized London shades make it easy for the owners to block out the light. The bed's headboard and footboard are based on a settee by the great English designer Robert Adam; the edging is fluted with oval medallions. The carpet is our homage to Wedgwood urns, vases, and plaques. THIS PAGE: In the master sitting room, a needlepointed gingham panel with silhouettes adorns a chair.

To our parents, Anthony and Mae Baratta and Herbert and Barbara Diamond, for teaching us to dream; and to Pauline Feldman, for showing us how to make them into reality — we dedicate this book to you.

A SINCERE THANK YOU

We would like to acknowledge the talent and effort of the countless people who helped bring this book to life.

To the creative team behind the book: Jill Cohen, the visionary who brought Diamond Baratta to print; Kristen Schilo, for her tireless efforts as our book editor; Doug Turshen, whose creative vision offered us something to strive for; Dan Shaw, our writer, whose beautiful words gave our interiors a voice; and Mary Louise Dudley for orchestrating everyone and everything in between.

A special thank you goes to: our clients, not all of whom could be included in this book, for trusting us with their dreams and allowing Diamond Baratta to make them into a reality; Jaime Magoon, for her invaluable design talents — she has long been our creative ally, whether it be in the office or for this book; Lois Chernin, for creating the exquisite needlepoint on the chair that graces this book's cover, and Ken DeAngelis, for upholstering the chair; Tria Giovan, for contributing her beautiful photographs; Nicholas Baratta, for being our in-house photo editor; Mikhail Rakovsky, for his generous architectural talent over the years; and Alan Mirken, for being more than a friend, and also a constant coach through the publishing experience.

To the editors and writers who have invited Diamond Baratta into the homes of their readers: Donald Albrecht; Dominique Browning; D. J. Carey; Doris Chevron; David Colman; Stephen Drucker; Cynthia Frank; James Huntington; Elaine Greene; Anthony Jazar; Jason Kontos; Marian McEvoy; Ann Maine; Mark Mayfield; Nancy Newhouse; Lisa Newsom; Nancy Novogrod; Mitchell Owens; Carol Prisant; Paige Rense; Mayer Rus; Margaret Russell; Anita Sarsidi; Suzanne Slesin; Doretta Sperduto; Carolyn Sollis; Newell Turner; Pilar Viladas; and Michael Wollaeger.

Diamond Baratta homes are testaments to the dedicated artists and artisans that we have had the privilege of working with. We cannot sing their praises enough: Eric Beare; the Bielecky family; Sarah Bruce; the Boyko family; Steven Cavallo; Eric Chappeau; David Cohn; Kevin Cross; Larry DiCarlo; Kenneth Kayel and the De Angelis family; Osmundo Echavaria; Charles Edwards; Paul Ferrante; Paul Flammang; Dora Helwig; Flemming and Finn Hegner; Tracy Gill and Simeon Lagodich; Perry Guillot; Gregory Gurfein; Brian Gracie; Isabel Glover; Les Goss; Jan and Wayne Jurta; Bronko Kmet; Adam Lowenbein; Anthony Monaco;

Anthony Mott; John Nalwaja and James Frances; Tom Newman; Michael Pell; Frank Pollaro; Jim and Dick Reeve; Steve and Marjorie Klein; Stanley Schoen; Tim Sheridan; Patricia Sullivan; Manny Theodosiou; Tony Wala; Andy Ward; William Wardell; and May Yung.

We extend our gratitude to the staff of Diamond Baratta, past and present. They have been a constant source of pride to us, and we count them as our extended family: Denise Ackerman; Mauricio Bedoya; Jon Call; Karin du Temple; Melonie Edwards; Courtney Gaylor; Gayle Jenny; Fran Keenan; Evelyne Merine; Joanne Miller; Arian Myrto; Carlos Perez; Jane Murphy Randol; and Nicole Waters.

To the people who have helped deliver the creativity of Diamond Baratta to the world: the Kravet family and Steven Elrod at Lee Jofa; John Stark, Steven Stark, and Rick Zolt of Stark Carpets.

And finally, to those we hold close: the Baratta family, the Diamond family, and all of our friends. Your continued encouragement and support inspires us every day.

CREDITS

YOUNG MODERNS pp. 8–9: Tony Baratta drawing photographed by Antonis Achilleos; pp. 10–23: Tria Giovan; pp. 24–31: Jason Schmidt; pp. 32–37: Minh & Wass; pp. 38–43: Antoine Bootz; pp. 44–53: Alexandre Bailhache, originally published in *House & Garden*.

FOLK ART pp. 54–55: Tony Baratta drawing photgraphed by Antonis Achilleos; pp. 56–65: Tria Giovan, reprinted by permission from *House Beautiful*, copyright © March 2003. Hearst Communications, Inc. All rights reserved; p. 66: Antonis Achilleos; pp. 67, 70–74: Tria Giovan, reprinted by permission from *Veranda*, copyright © July 2004. Hearst Communications, Inc. All rights reserved; pp. 68, 69, 75: Billy Cunningham; p. 76: Antonis Achilleos, pp. 77–85: copyright © Scott Frances / Esto, originally published in *Architectural Digest;* p. 86: Antonis Achilleos; pp. 87–97: Melanie Acevedo, originally published in *House & Garden;* p. 98: Antonis Achilleos; pp. 99–117: Tria Giovan.

BOLD THEMES pp. 118–119: Tony Baratta drawing photographed by Antonis Achilleos; p.120: Antonis Achilleos; pp. 121–125: Francois Dischinger, originally published in *House & Garden;* pp. 126–139: Tria Giovan; p. 140: Antonis Achilleos; pp. 141–147: Michael Mundy, originally published in *House & Garden;* p. 148: Antonis Achilleos; pp. 149–161: Pieter Estersohn, originally published in *House & Garden*.

MODERN PASTELS pp. 162–163: Tony Baratta drawing photographed by Antonis Achilleos; p. 164: Antonis Achilleos; pp. 165–171: Carlos Domenech, reprinted by permission from *House Beautiful*, copyright © January 2003. Hearst Communications, Inc. All rights reserved; pp. 172–181: Jonn Coolidge, reprinted by permission from *House Beautiful*, copyright © April 2000. Hearst Communications, Inc. All rights reserved; p. 182: Antonis Achilleos; pp. 183–193: Tria Giovan; p. 194: Antonis Achilleos; pp. 195–207: Tria Giovan, reprinted by permission from *House Beautiful*, copyright © July 2004. Hearst Communications, Inc. All rights reserved; p. 208: Antonis Achilleos, pp. 209–215: William Waldron.

NEW TRADITIONALS pp. 216–217: Tony Baratta drawing photographed by Antonis Achilleos; pp. 218–227: Matthias Petrus Schaller, originally published in *House & Garden;* pp. 228–243: Jason Schmidt, originally published in *House & Garden;* pp. 244–251: Colleen Duffley, originally published in *Traditional Home* magazine; p. 252: Antonis Achilleos; pp. 253–259: Tria Giovan; pp. 261–269: Tria Giovan, reprinted by permission from *House Beautiful*, copyright © October 2003. Hearst Communications, Inc. All rights reserved.

Bulfinch Press

Hachette Book Group USA
1271 Avenue of the Americas, New York, NY 10020
Visit our Web site at www.bulfinchpress.com

First Edition: September 2006

Library of Congress Cataloging-in-Publication Data
Diamond, William. Diamond Baratta Design/William Diamond and Anthony Baratta.
  — 1st ed.
    p. cm.
  ISBN-10: 0-8212-5736-6 (hardcover)
  ISBN-13: 978-0-8212-5736-4 (hardcover)
  1. Diamond Baratta Design, Inc. — Themes, motives. 2. Interior decoration — United States — History — 20th century.   I. Baratta, Anthony. II. Title.
NK2004.3.D53A4 2006
747.092'2 — dc22   2006002807

Designed by Doug Turshen with David Huang

MANUFACTURED IN CHINA